New Plays

From A.C.T.'s Young Conservatory

Volume II

THE YOUNG CONSERVATORY AT
AMERICAN CONSERVATORY THEATER

A.C.T.'s Young Conservatory is a professional theater-training program for young people ages eight to eighteen. The emphasis is on the training of an actor and the development of a young person in relationship to their world and to others. The program provides quality theater training for the beginner, exploring theater and acting for the first time, as well as advanced level study for the young person with previous experience. Classes are designed to develop imagination, concentration, working with others, exploration of character, development of technique in acting, and skills of both the body and the voice. Learning to respect people and the creative process are essentials in the program. Some students come to explore and discover, others come to define and refine their talent and technique to take them further in their goal to become a professional actor. The faculty are working theater professionals who are passionate and skilled in their working with young actors. The Young Conservatory seeks to empower young people to strive for excellence in their lives, while embracing an atmosphere of safety that encourages exploration. The training opportunities frequently extend students the opportunity to play the young roles in the professional company, learning firsthand from working artists. The Young Conservatory is particularly devoted to developing in young people an appreciation of theater in the making of a more human world, and in the importance of the place young people have in the future of the American theater. To this end, the Young Conservatory is a center for actor training for young people and development of new theater writing both by young people and by professional playwrights challenged to see the world through the eyes of the young. Critical thinking, feeling, and giving are cornerstones of this twenty-year program.

CRAIG SLAIGHT is the Director of the Young Conservatory at American Conservatory Theater. During the past seven years in this position, Craig has worked passionately to provide a creative and dynamic place for young people to learn and grow in theater arts. With a particular commitment to expanding the body of dramatic literature available to young people, Craig has published five volumes, *Great Scenes from the Stage for Young Actors, Great Monologues for Young Actors, Great Scenes and Monologues for Children, Multicultural Scenes for Young Actors,* and *Multicultural Monologues for Young Actors,* co-edited by A.C.T.'s Jack Sharrar. *Great Monologues for Young Actors* was selected by the New York Public Library as one of the outstanding books of 1993 for teenagers. Additionally, Craig began the New Plays Program at the Young Conservatory in 1989 with the mission to develop plays by professional playwrights that view the world through the eyes of the young. The first five are collected in a publication by Smith and Kraus publishers, *New Plays from the A.C.T. Young Conservatory Volume I.* Educated in Michigan in Theater and English, Craig taught at the junior and senior high school, college, and university levels, prior to moving to Los Angeles, where he spent ten years as a professional director (directing such notables as Julie Harris, Linda Purl, Betty Garrett, Harold Gould, Patrick Duffey, and Robert Foxworth). Since joining A.C.T., Craig has often served as Associate Director for main stage productions. In addition to the work at A.C.T., Craig is a consultant to the Educational Theater Association, a panel member for the National Foundation for Advancement in the Arts, and is a frequent guest artist, speaker, workshop leader, and adjudicator for festivals and conferences throughout the country. In August of 1994, Slaight received the President's Award from The Educational Theater Association for outstanding contributions to youth theater.

New Plays

From A.C.T.'s Young Conservatory
Volume II

Edited by Craig Slaight

Young Actors Series

SK

A Smith and Kraus Book

A Smith and Kraus Book
Published by Smith and Kraus, Inc.
One Main Street, PO Box 127, Lyme, NH 03768

Manufactured in the United States of America
Cover and Text Design by Julia Hill

First Edition: March 1996
10 9 8 7 6 5 4 3 2 1

Library of Congress Cataloguing-in-Publication Data
Prepared by Quality Books

New Plays from A.C.T.'s Young Conservatory Volume II / Craig Slaight
p. cm. Audiences: Ages 12-22
ISBN 1-880399-73-3

1. American drama--Collections. 2. Plays--Collections.
I. Slaight, Craig. II. American Conservatory Theatre.
III. Title: New Plays from American Conservatory Theatre's Young Conservatory.
PS
PN625.5.N49   1993   812'.5400835
QBI93-20017

For Carey Perloff and Helen Palmer,
who make all things possible

THE YOUNG CONSERVATORY
NEW PLAYS PROGRAM
AMERICAN CONSERVATORY THEATER

Embracing the need to develop new theater writing that sees the world through youthful eyes, the Young Conservatory began the New Plays Program in 1989, with the commission of *Ascension Day* by Timothy Mason. While the exploration focuses on the life-journey at a young age, the effort is the creation of plays offered for an intergenerational audience.

The principal design of the program is that an invitation is offered to an outstanding professional playwright to create a new play with a youthful perspective. The playwright is given no less than six months to create the first draft of the play, a play that is not restricted in size of cast, length, or thematic content or style. With the first draft in hand, the director selects Young Conservatory students based on the demands of the play and the strengths of the students' acting skills. Although the young actors (between the ages of eight and eighteen) play most roles in this program, guest adult professionals have taken roles when appropriate. The playwright comes to San Francisco for a minimum of two weeks for rehearsals, during which time script changes are incorporated in the rehearsal process. At the end of a five-week rehearsal period, public performances are given.

In addition to Mr. Mason, the New Plays Program has commissioned plays from such distinguished playwrights as Mary Gallagher, Joe Pintauro, Brad Slaight, Lynne Alvarez, and Pulitzer Prize–winner Paul Zindel.

Contents

Introduction

Continuing the Quest

By Craig Slaight

It seems like yesterday that we asked Timothy Mason to be our first playwright to "see the world through the eyes of the young" and come to San Francisco with a new play. In fact, it was 1990 and the New Plays Program was an experiment. Happily, the experiment was a success and we went on to create five plays in three years. Those plays are published in the first volume of *New Plays From A.C.T.'s Young Conservatory.* With this collection, we offer four new plays, each of which promises a long life in theaters the world over.

We have continued with our original mission, simply to ask the extraordinary professional writers to consider a look at the world through a youthful perspective. We make no requirement as to the length of the play, the number of characters, the theme or subject matter, or even the complexity of the technical demands of the play. Much like placing a blank canvas and pots of paint in front of the visionary painter, we invite the playwright to compose a theater piece that is limited only by a young point of view. Our early efforts had shown us that this basic invitation had offered the writer an unusual freedom, a release from the demands of a commercial formula, or from the dictates of producers who wanted plays that served tastes of the current trends in theater. We said "Dream! In your own manner, create a story told through the minds and voices of young people."

Perhaps even more essential to our training mission here at A.C.T. is that this experience offers young actors a special vantage point: learning acting by working with professionals to create a new character in a brand new play.

If we had only created the first volume of these exciting plays, we would feel that as a group of artists (playwrights, actors, and directors) we had accomplished a worthy body of work. I'm overwhelmed to sit here today and introduce the book before you, with firm conviction and belief in the plays within and an equal confidence that we plan to keep going. In fact, I've just returned from New York where I made the next invitation to a formidable playwright to come and create a new play with us.

One of the unique opportunities we had by continuing this work was the possibility to work a second time with writers who had been with us in those first few years. While we created deeper, more profound, relationships with Timothy Mason and Brad Slaight, we had the excitement of new illumination with plays from Lynne Alvarez, a dynamic, contemporary, theater voice, and the distinguished Paul Zindel, whose *The Effect of Gamma Rays on Man-in-the-Moon Marigolds* (a play written with the same point of view we were exploring) was awarded the Pulitzer Prize. The interest from playwrights of such stature, such specific and exciting voices, gave us needed challenge to attempt to meet one another's expectations.

When I first began this program, I knew at some point I would ask Lynne Alvarez to join us. This is a playwright with enormous breadth of vision and diversity in style. Lynne was eager to consider our proposal since for some time she had wanted to write a play that drew on her experiences as a young woman living in Mexico. Our invitation provided Lynne with an opportunity for such an exploration. *Eddie Mundo Edmundo* is the exotic, poetic, contemporary story of a young Hispanic American who travels to a remote fishing village on the Gulf coast of Mexico to find the essence of his heritage and, ultimately, a purpose in his life. Here, the expectations of two very specific actions within the same culture collide. Here, young and old grapple to understand one another while adhering to the core of their cultural convictions. Lynne framed the story in a most theatrical style. The protagonist, Eddie Sanchez, our eighteen-year-old from New York, is aided in his struggles by Edmundo, a strange young fisherman from the village with mutant features. Edmundo is perhaps the most haunting character we've seen in all of our commissioned plays and Lynne's play is rich in ideas, language, and passion.

Brad Slaight's *Class Action* is an intricate collage of scenes and speeches that depict the out-of-class experiences of high school students. For Brad, the truth is a blend of trouble and fun, pleasure and pain. As with his other plays, Brad was interested in looking at those interactions between young people that push past the cliché and embrace the unique. Finding the awkwardness of high school existence a highly charged pallete, Brad challenges our perceptions while still illuminating the truth. In *Class Action* the "jock" is revealed to be a sensitive poet, the school bully confesses to an intended victim his troublesome, violent, life at home, an unwed mother is revealed in a private moment in which she promises a better life for her soon-to-be-born baby, and a dull homework assignment becomes a lively fantasy. During the rehearsal process the company of young actors, guided by Brad and a talented director, Amy Mueller, explored twice as many scenes and speeches as appear in the final play. It was Brad's desire to look at as many different situations as possible before honing an evening framed in laughter and moments of profound sadness. The result is an unusual high school experience.

Timothy Mason was drawn to the late sixties, a time in our history that was fraught with conflict and turbulence, a time when teenagers were asked to identify their beliefs and stand up for them. *The Less Than Human Club* is a memory play in that it creates an event that requires resolution of a disquieted, earlier, time in life. To do this, Davis, the central character, must return to the pain and the pleasure of his junior year in high school. As Davis invites us to join him on his journey back, the play moves from the present to 1968 replaying scenes from that formative year and pushing him toward reconciliation with the unsettled past. Focusing on themes of deception and the tests of friendship and true love, *The Less Than Human Club* is a startling and moving picture of the turns taken when young and how such turns alter the course of our entire life. This is an ageless detailed journey. Indeed, the adults who saw the play were as lifted and crushed by the revelations in the play as the young people.

Paul Zindel was interested in how today's young people handle the bombardment of ideas and images from, seemingly, everywhere (television, magazines, billboards, music, fashion). He was also interested in the results of failed parenting on children. In no way did he seek a story of righteous young people wailing about inept parents. Rather, Paul chose to ask: What becomes of children when their parents face failure by running away? *Every Seventeen Minutes The Crowd Goes Crazy!* shows us what might be one step beyond divorce—a family of children abandoned by their parents. These are parents who have failed as players in a complex society and who prefer to handle that failure by leaving the family to become pleasure seekers. In this case, pleasure comes in the form of gambling at the trotting races and Native American casinos. The only communication with the children is through the family fax machine. Meanwhile, the children are left to determine how to go on. Can they hold out for a hopeful recovery and return of the essential Mother and Father, or should they push forward without them, questing for their own place in this mad world? Zindel's sardonic wit, ingenious use of language and highly theatrical style delivers a play as large as any Greek tragedy and as timely as today's newspaper.

Here, then, we offer four different, highly compelling, plays. You will no doubt nod your head in agreement, shake your head in disagreement, laugh, and weep, as you journey where we have been in the creation of this body of work. As always, I would encourage you to seek full productions. Plays are written to be PLAYED. To gain a full realization of this work, you really must play them and see them on the stage. I invite you to dig deeply into the pages that follow. When you have finished, I can promise you that we will return soon with more.

As with our last collection, we've included comments by each of the playwrights as well as some of the young people who first created these characters. If only we could capture the look in the eyes of these young people when they first encountered these plays. Now that is something worth preserving!

Craig Slaight
San Francisco
September, 1995

EDDIE MUNDO EDMUNDO

by Lynne Alvarez

BIOGRAPHY

Lynne Alvarez arrived in New York in 1978 planning to be a hot-shot poet. On a whim, she accompanied a friend to a gathering of Hispanic writers at the Puerto Rican Travelling Theatre. At 31, she had never had a thought of writing a play but was now hooked. Lynne wrote two plays under the auspices of Miriam Colon and the Puerto Rican Travelling Theatre: *Graciela,* which was presented at the Puerto Rican Travelling Theatre and *Guitarron,* which earned Lynne an NEA Fellowship and premiered in 1984 at St. Clements Theatre in New York.

Lynne was a member of New Dramatists for seven years where she wrote *Hidden Parts* (1981), which won the Kesselring Award in 1983. She also wrote *The Wonderful Tower of Humbert Lavoigent* (1983), which won two awards: The Le Compte De Nouey Award in 1984 and an FDG/CBS Award for Best Play, and, later, Best Production at Capital Repertory Company in Albany, New York in 1984/85. In 1984, the Actors Theatre of Louisville commissioned a one-act play which became the full-length play, *Thin Air, Tales from a Revolution. Thin Air* premiered at the San Diego Repertory Company in 1987 and won a Drama League Award and a Rockefeller Fellowship in 1988. Lynne won a second NEA Fellowship in 1989/90.

Lynne has also done commissioned translations and adaptations: *The Damsel and the Gorilla* or *The Red Madonna* by Fernando Arraval for INTAR in 1988; Tirso de Molina's *Don Juan of Seville* for Classic Stage Company (CSC) and an adaptation of Boccaccio's *Decameron* called *Tales from the Time of the Plague* for CSC as well. Lynne's adaptation of the children's story, *Rikki Tikki Tavi,* and a musical based on *The Pied Piper of Hamlin* called *RATS,* had their premier at the Repertory Theater of St. Louis in 1991 and 1992.

Most recently Lynne has been the recipient of a New York Foundation grant in 1994 and has created two plays for ACT's Young Conservatory including *Jaimie Brown* and *Eddie Mundo Edmundo.* She is the author of two books of poetry and her plays have been widely published and anthologized. Her most current play, *The Absence of Miracles and The Rise of the Middle Class,* is a murder mystery about class war in New York City.

AUTHOR'S NOTE

The Nautla I knew in the 1970s is probably gone now—infinitely changed from the small grassy town of stucco and "chamolote" homes I first saw when I arrived. When my dear director Craig Slaight and I sat down at the beginning of this production for *Eddie Mundo Edmundo* to find Nautla on the map of Mexico, I was shocked to see that a large highway and bridge now pass through it—perhaps obliterating the very roadside restaurant where I spent so many vacations with Chelo and her family.

And who knows what really happened to Mundo? Was he old when I met him or young? We never spoke. We only crossed paths once in the very early morning when the wood fires were just lit and the sun was crisscrossing the palm trees in the center of town. Who will ever know why he stopped—a looming figure swathed in white muslin—and lowered his veil to show me his deformed face? When I asked they told me he had a *hongo*, a fungus; they told me his name was Mundo, which I took literally as *mundo* meaning world, something wildly and improbably romantic. I only learned years later that Mundo was short for Edmundo—a perfectly proper name. But because of Mundo and that strange silent meeting—Nautla has always come to me as a complete and potent world full of secrets and mysteries I can only guess at. This play is my thank you and my good-bye to Nautla.

Lynne Alvarez

ORIGINAL PRODUCTION

Eddie Mundo Edmundo was commissioned and first presented by the Young Conservatory at the American Conservatory Theater (Carey Perloff, Artistic Director; John Sullivan, Managing Director), San Francisco, California, in August, 1993. It was directed by Craig Slaight; musical direction was by Maureen McKibben; costumes were designed by Callie Floor; design specialist was Cour Dain; music was by Jay Good; the assistant to the director was Peter Glantz. The cast was as follows:

Eddie	Paul Shikany
Mundo	Devon Angus
Chelo	Carmen Molinari
Alicia	Kristine Kuroiwa
Nyin	Jeffrey Bautista
The Woman with Blue Eyes	Jennifer Paige
Pipo, her boy	Nicholas Kanios

CHARACTERS

Eddie
Mundo
Chelo
Alicia
Nyin
The woman with Blue Eyes
Her boy Pipo

TIME AND SETTING

All action takes place in the 1970s in the village of Nautla, Mexico, on the coast of the State of Veracruz.

EDDIE MUNDO
EDMUNDO

ACT I
SCENE 1

Shafts of light as if early morning through palm trees. Mundo by the river, washing himself. Back to the audience. His pole and bucket against a rock. He is singing. He is wearing bracelets of silver bells and bells around his neck.

MUNDO: *(singing)* Ay de mi, Llorona, Llorona
   Lead me to the river
   Ay de mi Llorona Llorona
   Lead me to the river.
   Wrap me in your shawl. Llorona
   The wind is cold as winter
   Wrap me in your shawl, Llorona
   The wind is cold as winter.
   Ay de mi Llorona, Llorona
   Llorona of the present and past
   Ay de mi Llorona, Llorona
   Llorona of the present and past.
   If once I was a marvel, Llorona

Now I'm fading fast
If once I was a marvel, Llorona
My light is fading fast.

(As he is singing, Eddie walks in, hiking, a backpack, sneakers, jeans, Mundo stops singing abruptly.)

EDDIE: Hey. Sorry.

(Mundo is still.)

EDDIE: I'm looking for Nautla. The guy who dropped me off said to follow the river.

(Mundo doesn't respond.)

EDDIE: Should be just up the road, right? *(He slaps some flies.)* Damn! Yeah, well. Thanks a lot. I'll be going now.

(Mundo pulls up the muslin cloth he wraps himself in. He raises the hood and turns to stare at Eddie. His face is severely deformed. It looks as if it's made of melted wax. His skin has barklike patches on it. He says nothing.)

EDDIE: Shit.

(Mundo gets up. He is tall and thin. He covers his face with a light veil and approaches.)

EDDIE: Look my name's Eddie Sanchez. Maybe you know Chelo Sanchez—

(Mundo stops.)

EDDIE: She's my aunt. Maybe you knew my mother Tati?

(Mundo comes closer.)

EDDIE: Yeah, well my Spanish ain't so good. I'll just be leaving now.

(Mundo raises his arm abruptly and points up the road staring intently at Eddie.)

EDDIE: That way. I get it. She lives that way. That dirt road. Cool. Thanks. *(He starts off.)*

(Alicia comes with a bucket, calling.)

ALICIA: Mundooo. Mundo—oh!

EDDIE: Hey—hi! Good Morning.

(Alicia stares at him. Turns to Mundo and ignores Eddie.)

ALICIA: Mundo, we need at least a dozen claws. You know how Father Bernardo eats. And how many clams do you have, let's see.

(Mundo shows her the pail.)

ALICIA: All of those. I'll come back at noon.

(Mundo exits.)

EDDIE: *(after her)* Don't let me forget to say good-bye. Man, what is it—

no one talks around here? *(He starts off.)* This has got to be the fucking end of the world!

SCENE 2

Alicia is on the bridge. River sounds. Seagulls. A little boy and a middle-aged worn-looking woman arrive.

BOY: *(Looking at the river.)* Ooooooooh.

WOMAN WITH BLUE EYES: Keep back you idiot. Do you want the current to gobble you up?

BOY: *(Looking way up and turning around.)* The trees are so green and so quiet.

WOMAN: That's all you know! Look.

BOY: What?

WOMAN: There's a boa constrictor in those branches just waiting to wind himself around your scrawny neck and crush you to death. And there!

BOY: Where?

WOMAN: In those leaves. There's a nauyauque hiding. He'll drop on your back and bite you till you turn blue and die. Stay close to me. Things aren't what they seem.

BOY: I'm hungry.

WOMAN: *(Searches her bag and gives him a tortilla.)* Here.

BOY: It's so quiet. Do you like it? I like it. *(He eats.)* But mama, do you think...do you think. What about the wind, mama?

WOMAN: Keep your mouth shut. There's a village around here somewhere and I'll never get a day's work with you hounding me with your gibberish.

BOY: You won't leave me?

WOMAN: If only I could.

ALICIA: *(from the bridge)* Why do you talk to him like that?

WOMAN: Who are you to tell me how to talk to my boy?

ALICIA: Come here little boy.

(The boy goes to the bridge.)

ALICIA: I have a cookie for you.

WOMAN: Give him two. I need something sweet.

BOY: *(snatches the cookie)* Who are you?

ALICIA: Alicia.

BOY: I'm Pipo. Where do you live?

ALICIA: Here. In Nautla. And you?

BOY: Mama?

WOMAN: We live on our feet and on our backs. And now, I need work girl. I need a roof and food for my boy.

ALICIA: What do you do?

WOMAN: I wash anything clean. So! Do you know anyone who needs help? A home, a store, a ranch, a restaurant?

(The boy is walking back very careful. As if along an invisible line.)

BOY: Uh-oh.

ALICIA: *(to the boy)* Are you afraid to walk back? Here—I'll help you. *(She walks with him.)*

WOMAN: Help me and you help him.

ALICIA: He doesn't look like your son. You have blue eyes—like a cat's.

WOMAN: An indian with blue eyes invites nothing but trouble. What about the work?

ALICIA: Well, we might need help at the restaurant—the rainy season's over and people come to the beach. Go down this road and ask for Chelo Sanchez. She'll know what to say.

WOMAN: What is this blessed place again?

ALICIA: Nautla.

(The boy clings to her dress.)

WOMAN: Idiot, you're tearing my dress. Move!

BOY: If it moves, mama it'll sweep me away and I'll never see you again.

ALICIA: What's wrong with him?

WOMAN: How do I know? He's crazy, afraid of the air, especially the wind. *(She shoves him.)*

ALICIA: Don't do that!

WOMAN: He's no concern of yours.

ALICIA: Pipo—don't worry about the wind. Look at the birds. When the wind blows they face the wind and fly away. It helps them fly anywhere they want.

PIPO: No!

ALICIA: And today is a beautiful day. The sun's shining. Look at all the flowers. The air has never been so pure. *(She kisses the top of his head.)*

(The woman and Pipo leave.)

SCENE 3

Chelo's restaurant. Outdoor patio. Rough tables and chairs. Pots of flowers. Chelo sweeping, Eddie arrives.

EDDIE: Chelo Sanchez?

CHELO: Yes?

EDDIE: Aunt Chelo?

CHELO: Edmundo? *(She runs to him emotionally.)* Ay! Edmundo. *(They embrace and stay that way for a long moment. Eddie is moved too.)*

CHELO: Only now that I see you I know it's true. She's gone. Poor Tati. Little Tati. I should have been the first.

EDDIE: She's gone.

CHELO: Did she suffer? Was she in pain?

EDDIE: Yeah.

CHELO: Did she die alone?

EDDIE: Yeah.

CHELO: Like your grandfather. Just like papa.

EDDIE: No one called us. I went to visit. I found her. I walked in. It must have been right after she...It didn't even look like her, you know.

CHELO: In her illness—was your father by her side?

EDDIE: After a while he couldn't go in her room.

CHELO: Of course. *(She looks at him closely.)* You look like your father.

EDDIE: That's what they tell me.

CHELO: I pray you have your mother's heart. Here, sit. Do you want a beer? I want a beer. *(She disappears into the house and reappears with two beers.)* You like Mexican Beer?

EDDIE: Sure.
(She embraces him again and starts to cry.)

EDDIE: Auntie. Look. I brought you some things. She wanted you to have them. *(He opens his backpack and takes out a scarf.)*

CHELO: *(Takes the scarf and smells it.)* It still smells like her. Smell.

EDDIE: No. I got more pictures and a dress packed away. She didn't leave much.

CHELO: She didn't have much. But she had you.

EDDIE: Let's not talk about her okay? Oh—shit—one more thing. Here. *(He takes out a ring.)*

CHELO: She didn't want to be buried with her wedding ring?

EDDIE: Pop wanted to sell it. Maybe you could use it.

CHELO: I can use it. It's time me and your uncle got married. We've been fiancées for thirty years!

EDDIE: Thirty years?

CHELO: You're a good boy. Stay as long as you want.

EDDIE: I don't know what I want, auntie. Mom talked about Nautla like it was paradise. Man, I could use paradise right now. Nautla—Hey auntie—who's the man with the face like melted wax?

CHELO: Mundo. He's a fisherman. Why?

EDDIE: I'm here fifteen minutes and I've already seen the most grotesque human being ever and a girl who takes my breath away. Who knows what else might happen if I stay.

CHELO: You like girls.

EDDIE: Does the Pope pray?

CHELO: Edmundo.

EDDIE: Eddie.

CHELO: Eddie then—you should know—Men here are…very excitable. Very proud. Especially about their women. And if one doesn't have a gun, he has a machete. You have to be very careful about women here.

EDDIE: Sounds like home to me.

CHELO: I don't know New York City. But last week in Vega, your cousin, Ramon Flores, dragged his own daughter out of her house. Made her kneel and put six bullets in her head because she was unfaithful to her husband.

EDDIE: I get it.

CHELO: And that girl you saw with Mundo…

EDDIE: Yeah?

CHELO: Don't mess with her Eddie. She's our goddaughter. There's already a problem with her and a boy. She's very strong-willed. I promised her father I'd keep her here—safe—for a while. I don't want trouble in my house.

EDDIE: I'll respect your house, auntie.

CHELO: Maybe I'm putting the wood too close to the fire.

EDDIE: Who's the wood and who's the fire auntie?

CHELO: You're making a joke. It's not funny.

EDDIE: I can keep it in my pants.

CHELO: Did you talk like that to your mother?

EDDIE: (sings) In a small wooden boat on the ocean
    sailing sailing out to sea

Nautla my love, my darling
That's where I must be
that's where I must be.
(En un barquito de vela,
Voga, voga por el mar.
Nautla de mis amores
Tendre que llegar,
tendre que llegar.)

CHELO: Your mother taught you that.

EDDIE: Yeah.

CHELO: Your mother was too sweet. That was her trouble. And you—just don't be a bum.

EDDIE: Like my father.

CHELO: I didn't mean that.

EDDIE: Didn't you?

CHELO: Things happen.

EDDIE: Do you hate him so much?

CHELO: I'll tell you a little family history, Edmundo. Your mother was carrying you while your parents were still down here. Our father was dying then. All the daughters, we took turns spending the night helping him sleep through his pain. Every night, our mother would give us five thousand pesos to buy morphine for our father. His pain was terrible. One night, your father volunteers "Hey, I'll stay so you girls can get some rest". So nice. So thoughtful. We couldn't thank him enough and mama handed him the five thousand peso note as usual telling him what it was for. Your father kissed each one of us as we left and told us not to worry. That night, though, our papa never got his morphine.

EDDIE: What happened?

CHELO: What do you think? Your father met a local girl and wanted to play the big man. He bought tacos and chalupas and beer for her and her friends and guess who's money he used? Your grandfather lay twisting in bed with pain—all night. Now, do you still want me to answer your question.

EDDIE: No.

(Chelo kisses him.) (The woman with Blue Eyes enters. The boy and Alicia follow.)

WOMAN: Ah—an old woman kissing a young boy. I always thought it should be done in private, but what do I know—a poor ignorant woman looking for work. I can set tables, clean floors and dye them red once a month.

CHELO: I hope your work's cleaner than your thoughts.

WOMAN: I say what I see. I do what I'm told. A young girl—here she is— told me you might need a day worker.

CHELO: We could use one for a month or so. *(She winks at Eddie but puts her finger to her lips.)* Especially now that there's going to be a wedding. God help me.

WOMAN: God? God'll help you on your death bed. I'll help you now. I'm good. I'm not shy about what I can do. Even the saints want their candles lit.

CHELO: You can start now. You'll need to wash dishes. Bring the water in from the well. I like lemons in my wash water so the dishes smell clean.

WOMAN: That's easy enough.

CHELO: And there's a large basket of tortillas in the kitchen. When someone comes, you'll have to heat them four at a time over the burners without singeing them.

WOMAN: There should be good food at a restaurant.

CHELO: I'll give you forty pesos for two weeks and a bed for you both, and meals.

EDDIE: Hey—*(stoops to see the boy)* What's up midget?

ALICIA: His name's Pipo.

BOY: I like it here, mama. It's so still. *(He waits, listening.)* Will it last?

EDDIE: What's with this kid?

WOMAN: He wants to know if the work will last.

BOY: *(Happy, as if performing.)* The wind moves.
It's air. It's air.
The hot breath of animals
behind you
Beware.
I know. I've seen it.

WOMAN: It's nothing. Bad winds hit us on the road once. Trees fell and killed some people right next to us. Not this far away. There was blood I tell you. Now he's jumbled it all up in his head and he's cuckoo with it. *(To the boy.)* You're good at fetching water ain't you? *(To Chelo.)* He's stronger than he looks. Where do we put our things?

CHELO: I'll show you. The well's out back. You must want something to eat. *(She exits, they follow.)*

ALICIA: Who are you?

EDDIE: Eddie. Why didn't you talk to me before?

ALICIA: I didn't want to. Are you from New York City?

EDDIE: Yeah.

ALICIA: We have a saying—"Crazy as a goat in New York City." Is it like that?

EDDIE: What?

ALICIA: Crazy. Cars all over the place. Noise.

EDDIE: That's a pretty good description.

ALICIA: I'd hate it there.

EDDIE: I couldn't imagine you there.

ALICIA: Why not?

EDDIE: Give me fifty years and I'll tell you.

ALICIA: You think I'm ignorant?

EDDIE: No. No. It's just. Forget it.

ALICIA: Well. You don't belong here either.

EDDIE: Fine.

ALICIA: My name's Alicia. How old are you? I'm sixteen.

EDDIE: Old enough.

ALICIA: I have a boyfriend. My parents don't want me to marry him. I don't know why not. My mother married at fourteen. *(Waits for a response. There is none.)* That's why I'm here. He'll come and get me though. Soon.

EDDIE: Good. I wish you luck.

ALICIA: Doña Chelo told you not to talk to me, didn't she?

EDDIE: Sort of.

ALICIA: And you're afraid of me.

EDDIE: Give me a break.

ALICIA: You'd make an excellent priest, you know. Such self control. And so handsome…I always wondered why so many priests are handsome. What a waste. And they're embarrassed by everything. Nuns are never embarrassed. *(She looks at him.)* It's fun torturing you like this. Making you talk.

EDDIE: I ain't talking.

ALICIA: I heard your mother died. I'm sorry. I was trying to cheer you up. I'll leave you alone. Your name is Eduardo?

EDDIE: Edmundo. Eddie.

ALICIA: Oooooooooo.

EDDIE: What?

ALICIA: You have a namesake in the village.

EDDIE: Yeah, who?

ALICIA: I'll give you a hint. Neither of you talks. But at least he sings. *(Chelo enters.)*

CHELO: Alicia—the crablegs, girl! We need them for the Father's lunch. Go ahead.

ALICIA: *(Hugs her.)* I love you, Doña. *(She exits.)*

EDDIE: So auntie—what can I do? There must be something I can help with around here.

CHELO: No. No. This is your vacation. Eat, swim, do whatever you like.

EDDIE: Maybe I'll go swimming.

CHELO: Yes—but maybe not in the river. It looks peaceful enough. But the current is very bad. It can pull an ox under in a minute and he's gone.

EDDIE: I'll fish.

CHELO: Fish. Good. But not a high tide. The ocean rushes in and sharks swim up the river as far as a mile. They smell blood, it's all over.

EDDIE: Thanks. I'll just stay here for now. *(He gets out a paper and pen.)*

CHELO: You writing your father?

EDDIE: What?

CHELO: In the letter.

EDDIE: It's not a letter.

CHELO: Oh. *(She looks over his shoulder.)* English?

EDDIE: Yeah.

CHELO: It's so funny—a kid knowing so much English at your age. Look at that. Writing it as if it's nothing.

EDDIE: Yeah.

CHELO: Oh and there's a little matter I want to discuss with you.

EDDIE: She started the conversation, I swear to God.

CHELO: No, no, no. You gave your word. I believe you. This is about the ring and the wedding. Let that be our little secret for now.

EDDIE: No problem.

CHELO: Good. Oh—and Edmundo—we have to get your Uncle Nyin to confession. Soon. Maybe you could ask him to go with you sometime. Tomorrow.

EDDIE: I'm not religious, auntie.

CHELO: You can do me this favor.

EDDIE: I've never been to confession. I don't even know what words to use. Why don't you just ask him to go?

CHELO: I can't make that man see the need to. He's as full of sin as the next man. He spends half his nights and every Sunday drinking at La Napa's.

EDDIE: Maybe he feels drinking isn't a sin.

CHELO: La Napa is a prostitute. He has no business there.

EDDIE: Uncle Nyin doesn't know me. I don't think I'm the person to approach him on this.

CHELO: The fool. He only drinks there. His big feet are always on the floor when I go by. But he wants me to think differently. Other people do. They talk. I never hear the end of it. Now I'm only telling you this because you're Tati's son and I could always open my heart to her. But now…You see, it's urgent. Nyin must confess.

EDDIE: Why? Is he dying?

CHELO: Something sudden could happen.

EDDIE: Like a wedding?

CHELO: You never know.

EDDIE: Just tell him.

CHELO: He'll know.

EDDIE: Good.

CHELO: The day of the wedding.

EDDIE: This is fucked up, auntie.

CHELO: And what about being engaged for thirty years?! Nyin thinks it's romantic. I'll be fifty next month. I won't go to my deathbed unmarried and die in mortal sin for that man. And now with you children around, we have a responsibility.

EDDIE: I don't want to be involved.

CHELO: You're already involved. You're family. You brought the ring. I'm sure it was a sign from your mother.

EDDIE: Look…

CHELO: What? You think all family is, is a good meal together and that's it? You sit down, lick your plate and leave? No, no, no. If you want to be family, you're like snakes twisting together in a nest. You get warmth. You give warmth. If sometimes you're bitten, you take the poison and live through it. That way you all survive. So don't make me deny your mother's last wish for me. Take Nyin to confession. I'll make some excuse. Alicia'll go too. Nyin adores her. If she smiles, he has a good day. So you'll do it. Good. I'll have a talk with Alicia. And this? *(She picks up a bridle.)* I'll make the bridal lazo. We'll have baked red snapper and a big white cake. I'll let out my lace dress.

And one day, I'll just grab Father Bernardo and it's done. *(She looks heavenward.)* Tati, Tati—rest in peace.
(Chelo leaves. Eddie sits and writes.)

SCENE 4

Later. The Woman with Blue Eyes. She is cleaning the restaurant and her skirt is tied up revealing her legs. The boy is trying to hold on to her while she works.

WOMAN: A wedding, a wedding. What a joke! Stay out of my way boy. Can't you let go of my skirts! So young and wanting a woman's skirts.

BOY: But you're my mother. You're not a woman. And I love you.

WOMAN: I'm a woman, muchacho, and now I hate men. Hate them. Do you hear?!

BOY: Do you hate me then?

WOMAN: You're not a man yet. *(She pokes him in the groin.)* Though you've got the makings of a man. Anyway you're crazy and you're mine.

BOY: And I'll protect you. Always!

WOMAN: Right. The day a frog grows hair!

BOY: *(Happily he helps her straighten things.)* It smells like flowers here.

WOMAN: Flowers die too.

(Nyin enters dragging behind him the wired skeleton of a horse. He is a wiry little man in old, shapeless clothes with a straw hat with a hatband on it. He rarely smiles, but when he does, it surprises his whole face into a wonderful, mischievous grin. The Woman with Blue Eyes is bending over showing her legs. She does not see him. The boy goes directly to the horse and strokes it in wonder.)

NYIN: *(Coming up very close behind her.)* Now, what the hell do we have here?!

WOMAN: *(Jumps around and finds herself face-to-face with the skeleton. She shrieks.)* Jesus in heaven! What is that thing?!

NYIN: *(Taken aback by her appearance from the front.)* A walking rag.

WOMAN: *(Speaking of the horse.)* Ayy! A walking bone. And who are you?

NYIN: It's my house, damn it. Who are you?

WOMAN: I'm a hired woman.

NYIN: *(Examining her.)* You must have been a beauty once. Look at those blue eyes. I don't have to worry about you though. *(He takes off his hat and shows her the brim.)* That's snakeskin…see. Took it from the head of a boa constrictor.

WOMAN: So what's that to me?

NYIN: It protects me against the evil eye…blue, green, brown…even red ones.

WOMAN: If I had my eye on you, it would take more than a few snake scales to keep me away…Hah! *(She goes to touch him.)* You have dirt on your pants.

NYIN: *(Backing away.)* Don't touch me.

BOY: The wind ate the horse up, Mama. But he's very clean. He shines…

NYIN: Strange child you got there. Where's Chelo?

WOMAN: Your wife?

NYIN: My fiancée.

WOMAN: Ahhh, I see. So this wedding is for you?

NYIN: What wedding? No wedding. Being engaged is the most romantic time of our life. We wouldn't ruin it.

WOMAN: Your sweetheart seems feverish. She's talking lilies and camellias and so much lace. None of it white. I thought for sure the wedding was hers.

NYIN: Our cousins from Vega and Orizaba. They marry here all the time. They even come from Fortin de las Flores.

BOY: Can I have a ride?

NYIN: No.

BOY: Please.

NYIN: He can't hold you now. Old Frijol. Poor old Frijol…look how they wired him together so I could bring him home…*(He sits down and cries.)* Poor Frijol. Black as a bean. He was a born leader…He looks like Archbishop Rinaldo, don't you think?
(The boy laughs happily.)

NYIN: All the horses respected him. They'd fall into line behind him, trusting as babes bobbing their heads all the way to the glue factory…Damn. *(He wipes his eyes and nose.)* But he was old and lame and this time I left him to go through with the others…he turned one last time…he couldn't understand why I didn't come take him by the bridle and pull him away like always. *(Cries harder.)* Trusting to the last. I betrayed him.

BOY: *(Comforting.)* He's quiet now and pretty. I like him.

NYIN: *(To boy.)* Well it's over and done...now where shall I put him?

WOMAN: In the trash heap!

NYIN: He's good as new. Looks younger than ever...*(He carries the skeleton near the restaurant door.)* Maybe here...hmmmmmm...*(He moves him near the altar.)* How about here?...eh, boy? I can stand him right here and he'll be a witness for the wedding. *(He finds the bridle with flowers worked in.)* Well, look at this. Good old Chelo was making something special for Frijol after all...*(He puts it on the horse.)*

WOMAN: That's the bridal wreath for the bride and groom.

NYIN: Poor souls. They'll be harnessed together like two beasts.

WOMAN: And when it's your turn?

NYIN: Don't look at me! Chelo's a strong woman, but I do as I please. I'm a free man.

WOMAN: *(Brushing up against him.)* I like free men. Even skinny ones. Rather have bones against me than nothing at all.

BOY: *(Coming to Nyin worried.)* What's that smell on the wind? Do you smell it?

NYIN: No boy.

WOMAN: I've never been married, but I've had all the men that have caught my fancy, I can tell you...

NYIN: Who would fancy a hag like you?

WOMAN: A hag, eh? You'll be sorry you said that!

BOY: Mama...I think...the wind smells like blood!

WOMAN: Get away, boy!...

SCENE 5

At night. A full moon. Nyin and Chelo sitting at one of the tables.

NYIN: I don't like the woman you hired. The one with the blue eyes.

CHELO: I hired her for the boy's sake. And we need help with the wedding.

NYIN: So...

CHELO: Yes.

NYIN: Who is it after all that's getting married.

CHELO: You don't know them. A sweet young couple with stars in their eyes.

NYIN: I see. We'll make a lot of money on this…wedding?

CHELO: Enough.

NYIN: And what day did you say it was?

CHELO: My birthday. Don't you dare ask me the date. You better know it! Why are you so concerned?

NYIN: I don't like so many people in my house.

CHELO: One last time.

NYIN: I saw Frijol's bridal with flowers on it.

CHELO: I made it as an act of love.

NYIN: He'll never use it. Frijol was killed today.

CHELO: Today? Poor thing.

NYIN: I betrayed him. I betrayed him.

CHELO: We have more endings than beginnings at our age. Still…

NYIN: Betrayal is the worst sin of all.

CHELO: I'll be fifty on my birthday. Fifty. I feel everything I felt at eighteen. Bright colors make me cry and love songs sweep me off my feet.

NYIN: Yes. Yes. Time is passing. The bayou's drying up. My boat got jammed in the mangrove roots and I could barely get it out. I felt old.

CHELO: Do you want to marry me? Nyin?

NYIN: Of course I want to marry you. We're engaged, aren't we?

CHELO: When?

NYIN: When? Why? When do you want to get married?

CHELO: Before I die.

NYIN: You don't want to go and spoil it all, do you. After all—since when have we needed a church for what we want to do?

(He hugs her and she pushes him away.)

CHELO: There's children in the house now.

NYIN: You wouldn't want me to get married against my will would you?

CHELO: You were baptized, confirmed and received communion against your will—that never stopped you before.

NYIN: I need to take a walk.

CHELO: To La Napa's.

NYIN: To someplace with barrels of pulque, and music. Somewhere romantic.

CHELO: Do you love me Nyin? I love you.

(Nyin walks away into the darkness.)

NYIN: I wish Frijol were here. The world's coming to an end.

SCENE 6

Later the same night. Eddie writing. Alicia sitting at the other table. Pipo comes out.

PIPO: Who are you waiting for?

ALICIA: Ay!

PIPO: Couldn't you see me?

ALICIA: Yes of course, you silly. I was just thinking.

PIPO: My mother says she can't see me at night because I'm so dark. When I was little she tied a string from my wrist to hers at night so she wouldn't lose me. Why am I so dark?

ALICIA: Because your mother didn't wash you in a burro's milk—so you didn't lighten like some other children.

PIPO: I like your hair. It's springy. *(He plays with it.)* A man with a hat was here. He left his horse but you can't ride it.

ALICIA: You mean Frijol? It was that man's best friend. He told me.

PIPO: He told me too. Black as a bean, he said. My father was black too and my mother lost him in the dark.

ALICIA: You should go to bed.

PIPO: My mother's snoring.

ALICIA: Turn her on her side.

PIPO: Will you be here in the morning?

ALICIA: Yes.

PIPO: And the next one and the next one?

ALICIA: Yes you silly thing.

PIPO: *(He looks at Eddie.)* Are you two married?

ALICIA: No. Now go to bed. *(She kisses him.)*

PIPO: Good night.

ALICIA: Dream of angels so you'll dream of me. *(She laughs.)*
    (Pipo exits. Eddie looks at Alicia. She glances at him. He looks down. Alicia stares at him.)

ALICIA: Are you doing homework?

EDDIE: No.

ALICIA: Can I see what you're writing?

EDDIE: It's in English.

ALICIA: Oh. Is it a poem?

EDDIE: Sort of.

ALICIA: About me—sitting here in the moonlight, pensive and beautiful?

EDDIE: No.

ALICIA: Is it about your girlfriend back home with long golden hair and long golden legs?

EDDIE: I don't have a girlfriend.

ALICIA: Ahhh, Edmundo the priest.

EDDIE: You wouldn't be safe with the priests I know.

(They look at each other.)

EDDIE: So—when's your boyfriend coming for you?

ALICIA: In a month. The next new moon.

EDDIE: Does he love you?

ALICIA: He adores me.

EDDIE: But he'll go a month without seeing you.

ALICIA: He pleaded with me to run off. He swore he couldn't live without me. He cried. He raged like a bull. He said he'd cut me or he'd die if I didn't leave with him. But it was too dangerous. And what's a few more weeks.

EDDIE: You don't love him.

ALICIA: How can you say that!

EDDIE: You're not that anxious to see him.

ALICIA: Well once we're married, we'll be together every minute. That's it.

EDDIE: Don't get married.

ALICIA: I'm not like that. Once we're together, we have to get married. That's the way it's done. Especially if your family doesn't like your choice—you run away, you sleep together—then everyone in the family is yelling and demanding you marry as soon as possible. The men really get mad. Machismo is nothing to fool around with. Men here are very jealous.

EDDIE: Men there too.

ALICIA: That bad?

EDDIE: Yes.

ALICIA: Are you the jealous type?

EDDIE: No. Not me.

ALICIA: Miguel is. My boyfriend. I sneak to the post office to call him. I told him about you.

EDDIE: Jesus Christ. Why?

ALICIA: To make sure he'd come.

EDDIE: Thanks a lot.

ALICIA: Can't you handle yourself?

EDDIE: I can handle myself and three others, with one hand tied behind my back if I have to.

ALICIA: Now you sound like one of us.

EDDIE: We're not so different.

ALICIA: Really?

EDDIE: Really.

ALICIA: Tell me—sometimes—don't you feel that when someone tells you not to do something—that's the very first thing you want to do?

EDDIE: Yeah. Sometimes.

ALICIA: Me too.

EDDIE: Don't play with me. I don't like it. *(He continues writing.)*

ALICIA: Write about me.

(Eddie ignores her.)

ALICIA: You and I are taking Nyin to confession tomorrow. Did Chelo tell you?

EDDIE: She told me.

ALICIA: Will you confess everything?

EDDIE: I have nothing to confess.

ALICIA: I do. Good night.

EDDIE: Dream of angels—

ALICIA: So you dream of me. Write about Pipo. Why don't you?

SCENE 7

A college cafe. Two years later. Eddie taps a microphone.

EDDIE: Can you guys hear me okay? Great. Uh…yeah, well this poem's about a kid I met. I mean, I don't usually think about kids, but I always wonder where he is. I hope he's safe. The poem's called…uh… *"Pipo gets well".*
In a world so new
that many things had not
yet been named,
Pipo, the smallest,
almost died of delicacy,
every flutter of light
a heartbeat.

Once Pipo awoke delirious
and cried,
"Mama, why am I
so much darker
than the rest?"
"Ah", his mother sighed,
"I did not wash you
a burra's milk
so you did not lighten
like the others."
And Pipo awoke again
and pointed to things
asking, "What's this,
What's this?" until
the world had a name
for all things
even the smallest
and the darkest.

SCENE 8

Nyin, Alicia, and Eddie kneeling in a church pew. They whisper.

ALICIA: I can't believe it. She left. Hypocrite. She only took five minutes.
     I know for a fact she has more sins than that!
EDDIE: Maybe she just says etcetera.
NYIN: What? What are you saying?
ALICIA: Nyin—you can go now. That lady left.
NYIN: You go first.
     (Alicia gets up. Genuflects, crosses herself.)
ALICIA: I'm going to light a candle for my grandmother. You go. Go on
     now. Then you can show Eddie what to do.
NYIN: I don't know why you can't do it just as well.
ALICIA: He's a boy. There's things he can't confess in front of me I'm sure.
     Now go on. *(She gets up and exits.)*
EDDIE: Well?
NYIN: Go ahead. Go ahead.

EDDIE: Aunt Chelo wanted you to show me how to confess.

NYIN: Priests make me nervous. Anyway, I have nothing to confess.

EDDIE: But Uncle Nyin...

NYIN: I'm not a hypocrite.

EDDIE: What about...that woman?

NYIN: What?

EDDIE: La Napa?

NYIN: Now that's where we should go for confession. You can talk to La Napa like a man. She can keep a secret too. Don't look so shocked. There's nothing to it. Why don't you come to La Napa's with me? You're almost a man now—shit you're not a virgin are you? Ever had pulque—eh Don Edmundo? Bet not. You should try it. You'll like it there. I like it. I can take my shoes off and open my shirt. You'd get a kick out of La Napa—she's only a little thing—maybe four feet tall but can beat the shit out of most men. She stands on a table and beats her sons with sticks when they do wrong. They're big guys too, but they stand there and take it saying "No Mama, I'm sorry Mama." You have a lot to learn about Mexico, boy. Don't judge Mexico by all the poor people who come up to your country. We have skyscrapers. We have pyramids! We have blonds. Real ones. *(To Alicia offstage, gesturing.)* You go. You go first. *(To Eddie.)* That girl's an angel, what could she have to confess? Come on. We can leave now. She won't be but a minute.

EDDIE: It's important to Aunt Chelo that we all confess.

NYIN: Why?

EDDIE: La Napa?

NYIN: She's jealous? Good for her. It's part of romance, it keeps the heart alive. But I told you I have nothing to confess and I'll tell you why right now. For your ears only. In all these years—I've never touched another woman. Not La Napa. Not nobody. Don't get me wrong. I'm as hot-blooded as the next fella, but we're novios. We've been engaged for thirty years—why ruin a good thing? But shit. Thirty years without another woman. If you say a word—I'll deny it. I'll pull a knife. And if you think I'll go up there and admit that to some man in skirts—*(Nyin gets up.)* It's time to go.

EDDIE: You love Chelo—why are you ashamed?

NYIN: Are you stupid? For a man, virtues are vices! You coming?

EDDIE: No. I'll wait for Alicia.

NYIN: Be careful, boy. Don't start what you won't finish. In Mexico betrayal is the worst and only sin. Poor Frijol. *(He leaves.)*

EDDIE: *(Praying.)* It's not like that. I'm not like you, papa. I'm young. It's natural. Fuck!

SCENE 9

By the river. Just before dawn.

EDDIE: Is this the only time we could spy on him?

ALICIA: He comes at first light.

EDDIE: How do you know?

ALICIA: That's when the crabs come out. Shhhhhh.

EDDIE: *(Slapping at flies.)* Damn!

ALICIA: Shhhhhh.

(We hear bells. Mundo walks along the river with his pole and bucket. He pokes around quietly for crabs. We hear a goat bleat.)

MUNDO: Goat. *(He digs in his robe and fills his hand with something and holds it out to the unseen goat.)* Baby come, come. Here. *(He waits, the goat bleats. He goes offstage.)*

(Eddie and Alicia look at each other. Mundo returns, wipes his hands on his robe and continues looking for crabs. He laughs.)

MUNDO: My goat. My goat. *(He pokes in crevices and starts to sing a popular lovesong. He wanders off as he sings.)*

I know I still have time
I know it's not too late
I know our love is true
That love will be out fate
And in all the years I live
Every heartbeat that remains
I'll live to give you love
I'll kiss away the pain
With kisses strong and wild
Like the passions you awake
I know I still have time
I know it's not too late.

(Alicia and Eddie wait until the song fades.)

ALICIA: Was he singing to his goat?

EDDIE: Man, that was really sad.

ALICIA: I thought it was funny. All that for a goat.

EDDIE: Maybe he's in love.

ALICIA: Mundo? Ay, I hope it's not with me. How awful.

EDDIE: You pay him a lot of attention.

ALICIA: I talk to him. Maybe I won't talk to him so much now.

EDDIE: He's a leper.

ALICIA: But Aunt Chelo told me he doesn't have leprosy. Some fungus ate his face. Something like that. The clinic in San Rafael sent someone to see. But—he's not a leper. People think so, but he's not. It affected his voice. He can't speak. But singing comes easily. I don't know why. You should ask him.

EDDIE: I will. Do people hate him?

ALICIA: Mundo? No. He'll be at the dance next week.

EDDIE: Does he sing at dances?

ALICIA: When it's people he knows. Sometimes.

EDDIE: Does he drink? Does he eat? Crack jokes? What's he like?
    (Alicia shrugs.)

EDDIE: Will you dance with me at the dance next week?

ALICIA: Why not?

EDDIE: In front of Chelo?

ALICIA: In public at a dance there's nothing wrong.

EDDIE: And here? Now?

ALICIA: We shouldn't be here.

EDDIE: I know. Aunt Chelo.

ALICIA: My boyfriend. I'm forbidden. Or is that why you're here? Is it?

EDDIE: How about you? Why are you here?
    (They kiss. Lightly at first and then fully.)

ALICIA: *(Steps away.)* What a fool!

EDDIE: Try not to look so pretty and I'll try not to be a fool.

ALICIA: I'm the fool not you. I wanted to kiss you but now, I don't know what I want.

EDDIE: I do. *(He takes her hand and kisses her again.)*

ALICIA: What?

EDDIE: What what?

ALICIA: What do you want?

EDDIE: You. Now.

ALICIA: Really?

EDDIE: Yes.

ALICIA: Okay. *(She unbuttons her blouse.)*

EDDIE: No. Wait. I'll be killed! You'll be killed! We'll be murdered in our sleep!

ALICIA: My boyfriend's two hundred miles away on an oil rig. Who would kill you?

EDDIE: It's a serious matter. Uncle Nyin…

(Alicia gives him a look.)

EDDIE: Okay. All right. Maybe he wouldn't kill me—but if Chelo ever knew. If she ever found out. I could never come back.

ALICIA: Were you ever going to?

EDDIE: No. I don't know.

ALICIA: Don't.

EDDIE: Why?

ALICIA: I could never be alone with you if I ever thought you'd be coming back.

EDDIE: That's crazy.

ALICIA: I know. *(She touches his face.)* You have the face of an indian.

EDDIE: I have my father's face.

ALICIA: So smooth. It doesn't tell me you're American. It doesn't tell me anything—except when you smile.

EDDIE: What does it tell you then?

ALICIA: My magic worked. I bought three candles from La Napa and said some special words when a cloud passed over the moon and see, you're here! I conjured you up.

EDDIE: I don't believe in that.

ALICIA: I do. It works every time.

EDDIE: How many times have you done this?

ALICIA: Once. You're the first. Now swear to me you won't come back.

EDDIE: But why?

ALICIA: If we were together and you left I would be so sad. If you came back, but not for me—I think I'd die.

EDDIE: It's stupid to swear to anything.

ALICIA: I'll swear first. I swear I'll never follow you. I'll never search you out. I'll never know your street, or your father, or your room, or your friends, or your life, or your death when it comes.

EDDIE: My father betrayed every woman he ever knew.

ALICIA: So?

EDDIE: It would be so easy to promise you anything—everything right now. So very easy. *(He kisses her.)*

ALICIA: Then do it. It would be easy to believe you.

EDDIE: I'll stay this summer and never come back to Nautla.

ALICIA: Ever.

EDDIE: Never.

(They stare at each other.)

ALICIA: Maybe we shouldn't be alone here now.

EDDIE: Yes, we should. *(He draws her to him.)*

SCENE 10

The Woman with Blue Eyes and the boy by the river.

WOMAN: *(Slapping herself.)* These flies. *(Looking around.)* How should I know where the girl is? She doesn't do half the work I do! Come here and give your mother a big hug.

PIPO: *(Finds Mundo's bells.)* What are these? *(He moves the bells so they ring. He puts them around his wrist.)*

WOMAN: Let me see those! Ayyy, take them off quickly. They're the leper bells. Take them off I say! *(She rips them off the boy and throws them in the river.)*

PIPO: No they're pretty. No.

WOMAN: I threw them in the river. I saved your life. They're leper bells.

PIPO: Do they call the wind up Mama?

WOMAN: They're from a sick man with skin like tree bark and no face. A leper, a leper. Do you hear me?!

PIPO: A leper.

WOMAN: Child are you so backward you don't know what a leper is?

PIPO: No.

WOMAN: Why do you think they're run out of villages and made to wear bells? They're the walking dead!

PIPO: Dead?

WOMAN: Carajo! Do you want to marry?

PIPO: Yes.

WOMAN: No woman will touch you if you've touched a leper...do you want children?

PIPO: A hundred.

WOMAN: They'll be born monsters and their skin will rot and boil off if you're touched by a leper.

PIPO: *(Looking into the river.)* Mama—the bells! I see them—spinning and spinning and spinning.

WOMAN: Keep away from there idiot. Imbecile. You could drown and I'd never know it!

PIPO: Mama! Mama! Look!

WOMAN: If you ever see a leper, call me. I'll chase him away. Let's go back.

PIPO: Mama—look! The river's turning green.

WOMAN: *(Comes to look.)* The ocean's coming into the river. It's high tide. Watch out for sharks.

ACT II
SCENE 1

The park: a huge mural of Juarez and Zapata. Dance music: Merengue.
We see Nyin and Chelo dancing. Pipo and Alicia. The Woman with
Blue Eyes is smoking. Everyone is dressed up. Nyin is a bit loaded. Eddie
is standing there. Nyin comes over.

NYIN: Viva Mexico! Viva. Epale—*(He does a few dance steps.)* Come on
  boy—dance, dance.
CHELO: Come on, dance with me Edmundo. This old woman can dance.
  (Nyin dances with Alicia.)
CHELO: You dance good. Dance with all the girls—see them whispering
  over there—Ay look, Diana elbowed the girl next to her and won't
  look at you now. Go. Give her a thrill. Ask her to dance.
NYIN: *(Staggers over with Alicia.)* This young girl is killing me—*(He takes*
  Chelo's hand.) I want to die in your arms. Come on Chelito. Leave
  the young ones alone.
  (They dance off.)
NYIN: Slowly but we'll get there.
ALICIA: *(Waves offstage.)* Adios Pelon. *(To Pelon offstage.)* Me? Sure! *(To*
  Eddie as she leaves.) Dance, dance. They're watching!
EDDIE: I'm fine.
ALICIA: Coward. Then hold this. *(She gives him her sweater. She laughs*
  and leaves.)
  (Eddie wanders to one side. The music fades. He presses the sweater to
  his face and breathes in Alicia's perfume. Chelo all perspiring comes over
  laughing.)
CHELO: Don't be so selfish. Give the girls a break!
EDDIE: I'm perfectly happy Auntie.
  (We hear Nyin yell offstage.)
NYIN: Viva Mexico!
CHELO: Life is harder here than you think!
EDDIE: Viva Mexico. Ay Auntie—this music. There's no love songs like
  Mexican love songs. The States are dry as toast—my mother always
  said that. She said it's sad to be a Mexican without Mexico.
NYIN: *(offstage)* Viva Mexico!
EDDIE: She made my parents poor; she forced them out she broke their
  hearts—but they loved her. And I love her for them. Viva Mexico!

CHELO: Something's happened to make you feel all this "love".

EDDIE: I'm happy, that's all.

CHELO: Yes.

EDDIE: What?

CHELO: Tell me—why is it that you and Alicia chatter, chatter all the time and now, tonight you hardly speak. You never dance. You barely look at each other except for a short hot glance when you think no one's watching.

EDDIE: She's a beautiful girl.

CHELO: So is Diana.

EDDIE: I haven't asked her to dance either. Auntie, come on—don't worry…

CHELO: Nyin and I are to blame. We've set a bad example. We've been living selfishly. That has to end.

EDDIE: Dance with me. You dance like a girl of eighteen. You dance like you have stars under your feet.

CHELO: This is getting dangerous. You talk like an angel. Alicia's radiant and laughs too much. We have the ingredients for a tragedy. And how can I stop it if Nyin and I are living in sin. I'll settle this tonight. *(Chelo sees Mundo.)* Mundo—poor soul. You're invited to a wedding. Next week. There'll be lots to eat and drink. And two old people dressed like a bride and groom. *(She exits.)*

(Pipo and the Woman with Blue Eyes dance by. Pipo goes up to Mundo curiously.)

PIPO: Are you a man? Are you a woman? I can't see your face.

(The Woman with Blue Eyes steps between them. She forms a cross with her fingers and holds it up to him.)

WOMAN: Spirit be gone! Spirit be gone!

EDDIE: He's harmless.

WOMAN: He's a curse. *(To Mundo.)* Stay away from my boy!

EDDIE: Leave him alone.

WOMAN: I will if you dance with me. I used to be the best dancer in San Rafael.

(Alicia comes into view.)

EDDIE: Sorry. I have things to do. *(He takes Alicia's arm.)* Dance with me.

ALICIA: I thought we weren't going to be together tonight.

EDDIE: It doesn't matter. Chelo knows. Keep smiling.

ALICIA: What will we do?

EDDIE: To hell with everyone. Dance with me. Closer. Closer.

(They dance.)

EDDIE: Chelo doesn't know everything. Just a little. Kiss me.

ALICIA: No. Not here. Let's dance.

EDDIE: Kiss me. I'm dying to kiss you. I can't be this close without kissing you.

ALICIA: Don't. People are looking at us.

(Eddie whirls her around faster, closer. His face in her hair.)

EDDIE: Who cares?! I'm crazy about you. Let them all know!

ALICIA: *(Pushes him away.)* Do you want to get us killed!

EDDIE: Come on. Who's going to kill us for a kiss?

ALICIA: My boyfriend's coming for me tonight!

EDDIE: What!? What are you talking about?

ALICIA: He's coming for me tonight. Look at the moon.

EDDIE: What about it?

ALICIA: It's the first new moon in August. He said he'd come.

EDDIE: So have you talked to him about us? Have you told him things are different now?

ALICIA: Are you crazy? Nothing's different. He'll ride up on a horse and I'll ride off behind him.

EDDIE: You didn't talk to him.

ALICIA: We arranged it a long time ago.

EDDIE: And you were just going to disappear?

ALICIA: Yes.

EDDIE: Alicia. You can't do this!

ALICIA: Why? Will you fight for me? Will you love me forever? Please!

EDDIE: You bitch!

ALICIA: We're engaged.

EDDIE: Have you slept with him?

ALICIA: And if I had—would you drop me as if I were a leper? *(She sees something.)* Ay!

EDDIE: What?

ALICIA: Miguel! *(She runs off.)*

(The Woman with Blue Eyes approaches Mundo menacingly.)

WOMAN: Get away.

(Mundo faces her.)

WOMAN: You're filth. Disease. You're not a man. You're not even an animal, a beast. You're…you're the rotting bark of a tree! Do you hear me? A tree.

(Mundo reaches out to grab and shake her. She steps away.)

WOMAN: If you touch me I'll cut your heart out and kill your little goat!

(Mundo exits.)

SCENE 2

Alicia walking. Mundo enters very agitated.

ALICIA: Oh it's you. Thank God. Walk with me a bit.

(Mundo goes in and out of the foliage ringing his bells and then listening. Finally he rings them and the goat bleats. He is relieved. He stands still and breathes deeply.)

ALICIA: You lost your goat? I'm glad you found him. Does he have a name? He loves you. He follows you everywhere. Believe me— you're better off with goats.

MUNDO: *(Turns abruptly to face her.)* No.

ALICIA: I just meant—when you fall in love, people feel free to ask you to give up your entire life, as if they were asking the time of day. I don't know what to do. I'm stepping off a cliff. I'm dying. I'm lost. You must be past all that. Like Nyin and Chelo. You see things with a clearer eye and a calmer heart. I wish I could be like that now.

MUNDO: *(angry)* I'm twenty-five.

ALICIA: What is it? What's the matter?

MUNDO: *(furious)* I'm twenty-five.

ALICIA: Oh. You're young. How terrible. *(She reaches out to him to soothe him.)*

(Eddie rushes in. In the excitement of the moment, they forget Mundo's presence.)

EDDIE: Alicia!

ALICIA: Why did you follow me?

EDDIE: Are you kidding? I'd follow you to the end of the world.

ALICIA: Fool! Do you have a machete? A gun? This isn't a game.

EDDIE: What are you going to do? Let Miguel come drag you away by the hair and fuck you so you have to get married. *(He grabs her.)* I could do that too.

ALICIA: *(Twisting away.)* You probably could.

EDDIE: You feel something for me. I know it.

ALICIA: Yes.

EDDIE: Don't go back. Stay here with me. *(He takes her hair in his hands.)* I'll stay here with you. I have to. I'm caught in your hair.

(They kiss. Mundo watches, then exits.)

ALICIA: I never slept with him.

EDDIE: Shhhhhh.

ALICIA: He's nineteen.

EDDIE: I don't want to hear.

ALICIA: I want you to hear. You should know.

EDDIE: No.

ALICIA: His name is Miguel. You should know his name. He works in Poza Rica in the oil fields. He's thin. He comes to me after work, his shirt black with oil. His hands are rough and burned. We walk down the road and the back of our hands touch. That's enough. His house is one room with painted brick and he has a brand new stove. He'd tell me all about it. His life. He would share his whole life with me. And I know what kind of life it is. I would be his wife and stand in the mornings in a loose dress waving to him, the roof would be made of palm leaves and the floor cement. I could count on him and he could count on me. We know the same songs. He hardly smiles, but when he does—it's like the sun rising. He has an open smile. If I stay with you. I'll close it.

EDDIE: Stay with me. I want you so bad.

ALICIA: If I hurt him like this I can never go back.

EDDIE: Why would you have to go back? Do you love him?

ALICIA: How did this happen? A month ago I didn't know your name.

EDDIE: I know.

ALICIA: And a month from now?

EDDIE: I'll make you forget everyone you ever knew.

SCENE 3

Chelo's restaurant patio. Tables and chairs overturned. Nyin stands near the skeleton of Frijol with a gun.

NYIN: *(to Frijol)* I tell you Frijol. It's a good thing you're dead. You're free of all this craziness. Drink, girls, love, tears, rage. And for what? Shit. One boy a maniac waving a pistol over a girl he can't find; another chasing after a girl he can't catch. Now I have to worry about—let's see—*(He counts his fingers.)* Three people, four counting Chelo who'll have a stroke when she sees all this. And Miguel is wild. He's crying like it's ripped out of his heart. Ay what torture it is to be young. If I were young again I couldn't live through it.

Thank God Chelo and I are in our quiet years. Chelo's sturdy as a rock. And look at you and me. You're a bag of bones and I'm a sack. Ah well. *(He begins to clean up.)* How many days did we walk down these roads you and me with the sun beating on our backs like a live flame? I never thought those days would end. And you, my friend never thought at all. It was enough to be together with dust in our mouths taking one step and then another. Doing one thing and then another. I'd brush you, you'd spill my coffee over. If I felt bad, you knew it. You'd push me with your nose until I walked into a fence and laughed. I tell you—that's how things should be. Nothing is above the love of a man for his horse—so much is below. And then, then, I betrayed you, my simple trusting friend. I led you like a lamb to slaughter—except you were a horse. I miss you Frijol. But you're damn lucky—getting old isn't a bag of tricks either. The door closes. The tomb yawns open.

(Chelo enters.)

CHELO: Nyin. What happened?

NYIN: Chelo?

CHELO: What've you done? Are you drunk? Why are you holding your rifle?

NYIN: Miguel was here looking for Alicia.

CHELO: What did you tell him?

NYIN: I told him he'd wear out his heart and no woman is worth that! But he wasn't in the mood to listen. He'd been drinking. First he wanted to shoot me. He kept saying "I might as well be dead. There's no greater glory than to die for love!". It would have been funny but he meant it. And he was drunk. Then he threw up and said "My love's gone to hell!" and left.

CHELO: Where's Alicia?

NYIN: I thought she was with you.

CHELO: No. No, she left the dance a long time ago. And Eddie? Where's Edmundo?

NYIN: God knows.

CHELO: Ay no! Does Miguel have his gun?

NYIN: Yes. And he's furious.

CHELO: God in Heaven. You were merciful in never giving us children.

NYIN: I'll go find them.

CHELO: Hurry.

NYIN: *(Checking his rifle.)* I've never shot a man before.

CHELO: It won't come to that.

NYIN: Men have been shot over who goes through a door first. And if Miguel finds them together…the world's full of stupidity. *(He exits.)*

SCENE 4
Eddie and Alicia are lying on the ground kissing. We hear the bushes swish. Alicia sits up suddenly.

ALICIA: Did you hear that?

EDDIE: *(Gets up to investigate.)* Shhhhh.

ALICIA: Get a branch! Get a stone!
   (Nyin enters.)

EDDIE: Uncle Nyin!

NYIN: *(Looks at Eddie, then at Alicia on the ground.)* Miguel was at the house.

ALICIA: *(Springs to her feet.)* Miguel? What did you tell him?

NYIN: He wrecked everything looking for you. Go help Chelo clean up. Now!

EDDIE: She's staying with me until he leaves.

NYIN: And you'll protect her?

EDDIE: Yes.

NYIN: Get out of my way. I don't have time for foolishness. You don't know what's going on here.

EDDIE: Careful Uncle. I know more than you think. A lot more.

NYIN: Get to the house Alicia. You've caused enough trouble with that poor boy Miguel, and now you've encouraged this little puppy here until he's pissing all over himself trying to please you. I've had enough. Go home.

ALICIA: Eddie—I have to. I'm sorry. *(She exits.)*

EDDIE: You can't deal with me like that.

NYIN: No?

EDDIE: No. I wouldn't let my father and I won't let you.

NYIN: We'll settle this in the morning.

EDDIE: Now. I mean it.

NYIN: All right. So?

EDDIE: I'll marry her. I'm staying.

NYIN: You're staying. In Mexico. In Nautla.

EDDIE: Yeah. What about it?

NYIN: And what will you do—find old horses and take them to the glue factory like me? Hunt for snakes and alligators in the swamps like me?

EDDIE: If I have to.

NYIN: This has gone farther than I thought. You must be completely crazy! Can you fish? Can you mend boats? Can you hunt? Can you trap? Do you have a gun or a net? Will a big American boy like you break your back for two centavos and a cold tortilla picking coffee or mangoes? Do you have a truck? A license to teach? Are you a magician creating jobs where no one else can find them? You want Alicia to be a maid while you look for work? Think boy—are we all so stupid that we head north for nothing? We give our work cheap to the gringos for nothing? Tell me—who in your life do you know who comes south looking for jobs, for wages, for work, for life? Everyone goes North—to the States. Have you lost your mind? I don't know why I'm even trying to talk to you. When the post office opens in the morning I'll call your father.

EDDIE: I won't go.

NYIN: You're a boy—you'll go.

EDDIE: Who are you to talk? You ran away with Chelo at eighteen. I'm eighteen.

NYIN: I knew these swamps like the palm of my hand at eighteen. Rich men from Puebla and Orizaba knew my name. I'd take them for anacondas and alligators and turtles as big as truck tires. They paid me in cash. At eighteen I already had a name. People looked me up.

EDDIE: You have a name now too. And it's "Fool"…

NYIN: Take that back.

EDDIE: Ignorant fool.

NYIN: Even though you're American—I can't excuse that. Take that back, son.

EDDIE: No. You know—my father may be a fuck, but he had some good advice. He always told me—"If you throw a punch, make sure it hurts."

NYIN: Don't ever call a man a fool down here.

EDDIE: What would you call a man whose woman plans an entire wedding—invites the guests, orders the food, calls in the priest without bothering to tell him he's the one to be led down the aisle to the altar as the groom?

NYIN: Wait. Wait. What's this?

EDDIE: Why do you think Aunt Chelo needs you to confess now—after thirty years? It's for your wedding mass.

NYIN: I can't believe it.

EDDIE: She's betrayed you.

NYIN: No.

EDDIE: Wake up. Everyone knows but you. And they're all waiting to laugh.

NYIN: What me the fool? Led like a lamb to slaughter. To hell with that!
(He exits.)

SCENE 5

Alicia and Chelo at the restaurant. Cleaning up.

CHELO: Are you happy?

ALICIA: Why should I be?

CHELO: You have two men wild about you.

ALICIA: What good is that? I can't stop thinking about Eddie.

CHELO: And Miguel?
(Alicia shrugs.)

CHELO: It happened so quickly. Too quickly.

ALICIA: When the river rises it rises—whether it's from one storm or a week of rain. It sweeps you away.

CHELO: I tell you Alicia. These men. I don't know how they do it. It's something they're born with. They're so convincing. So sure. Even as little tiny things. Their dreams seem so powerful. We come to believe they're our dreams. They're always so clear about what they want; they want a horse; they want a shirt; they want hot peppers, but not the ones with veins; they want a new pistol and they want you all in the same breath. What do you want?

ALICIA: I want to see what happens, Doña. Whatever that is. I want to be swept away.
(Nyin enters. Angry. Strides by them both.)

ALICIA: Where's Eddie?

CHELO: Nyin?

NYIN: Where's my good shirt?

CHELO: Why?

NYIN: I want it.

CHELO: Now? Are you crazy?

(Nyin exits into the house again. Chelo follows. Alicia exits to find Eddie. The stage is empty for a moment. Nyin comes out, his white guayabera unbuttoned, putting on lots of cologne.)

CHELO: Nyin talk to me.

(He continues to splash on cologne.)

CHELO: What's wrong? What are you doing?

(He glares at her. He hands her the cologne. He starts to exit.)

CHELO: Where are you going?

(He goes to Frijol and kisses him.)

NYIN: Hunting. *(He exits.)*

SCENE 6

Eddie in the dark. We hear bells.

EDDIE: Mundo—if you're out there. Forget it! I ain't in the mood for your little games or whatever—you hear what I'm saying? You know—you should take a hint. Aren't you sick to death of being an outsider, a freak show? See that's what I mean. You understand what I'm saying. So answer!

(Mundo steps into the light.)

EDDIE: Act human. You know you got a problem, but in my humble opinion you make it worse. You act so damn freaky. You dress like a...swami or something. You don't talk. You can talk. I heard you. Me and Alicia heard you talking to your goat. So what's wrong with people? *(He laughs.)* Yeah, yeah, the hundred thousand dollar question. People. Here I am giving you advice and I'm poison wherever I go. Just like my old man. I mean, I got here and I figured "home", you know. Everyone looks like me. The mayor, Nyin, maybe you, if you weren't so screwed up. It don't help. Here, I'm a dumb gringo. Back home I'm a dumb Mexican. Man...I mean it's not all like that. My neighborhood's pretty cool. You always hear about all this crime on the street, but I feel pretty safe. You go out four in the morning, the lights are on, people're hanging out. If I'm short on money—Tony—the guy at Mimi's'll always spot me a slice of pizza. New

York. New York—Hey—you'd love New York. Let me tell you, it's got a bad rep, but it's great. Nobody'd even give you a second look. You should see what's walking around the streets of New York! No offense. I could see you there. But Alicia—what could I do with Alicia in New York? If anyone so much as spit out the word "spic", I'd kill them. I'd be arrested for homicide. "Crazy as a goat in New York City"—that's the saying? Can you imagine your little goat there—traffic zooming around, horns blasting? No way. No way. And Alicia with that face like an open book. Like a...Like a sun. Like a saint. I wouldn't even want the fucking putrid air to touch her. So, which is the worst crime against humanity—taking her there? Or staying with her here?

(Eddie buries his face in his hands. Mundo drops his stick. His bells ring. He pats Eddie's shoulder. Perhaps to comfort him.)

EDDIE: The last thing I need is pity from you! *(He strikes Mundo's hand away.)*

MUNDO: Yes. *(He leaves.)*

EDDIE: Hey. I'm sorry. I'm sorry. You caught me off guard. Hey man, I'm sorry. It's not like that.

SCENE 7

The bridge. The Woman with Blue Eyes and her boy are coming home from the dance. The boy is humming. He holds up his fist.

PIPO: Look, mama—the stars are as big as my fist.

WOMAN: Then why is it always so dark on the road?

(We hear bells and the bleating of a goat.)

PIPO: Who's that?

WOMAN: He better not come close to me. I'll know what to do with him.

(A dark figure, Nyin appears on the bridge.)

WOMAN: Who's that? Can you see?

PIPO: It's the man with the hat.

WOMAN: *(Going up to Nyin.)* Well, well. Had too much to drink?

NYIN: Worse. Not enough.

WOMAN: You need to get drunk?

NYIN: Yes. Is the dance over?

WOMAN: The dance is over. The beer is packed. Of course—there's more than one way to get drunk and lose your senses.

NYIN: There is—eh?

WOMAN: You know it too.

NYIN: You mean mischief.

WOMAN: Well I ain't dead yet. Too bad you are.

NYIN: What do you mean?

WOMAN: Thirty years with the same woman. You're as good as married.

NYIN: I'm still a free man!

WOMAN: Not as free as all that.

NYIN: You'll be sorry you've spoke to me like this.

WOMAN: I think I'll be very happy that I've spoken to you like this. *(She moves very close.)* And you'll make me even happier—isn't that so?

NYIN: What about the boy?

PIPO: Did you get married mother? Was it beautiful?

WOMAN: Shut up. Shut up. You're speaking nothing but dribble. Follow this path—straight and tell Doña Chelo to put you to bed.

PIPO: No.

WOMAN: I'll be right along. I have to make sure this man isn't dead. It's very serious business. Now get along.

PIPO: But the wind, Mama! What if. . .

WOMAN: If you don't go I'll whip you till you can't sit down. You have to grow up sometime. A few steps alone'll help you on your way. Now git!
(Pipo leaves. Nyin grabs her arm.)

WOMAN: Wait. Wait up. God, when you blood heats up it boils.

NYIN: I've got the blood of conquistadors running through my veins. *(He pulls her along.)* Damn you're strong.

WOMAN: I'm as strong as some men. I wish I were a man.

NYIN: I'll make you glad you're a woman.

WOMAN: *(Holds up her skirts. Nyin is hidden. She looks like a bird of prey.)* Well get on with it. Get on with it. I like a good strong man who makes me feel like I've been hit by a thunderbolt.

SCENE 8

Blackout. The boy walking in the dark. He hears a noise, stops.

PIPO: *(Looking around.)* Mama? Mama?

CHELO: Who's there?

(The boy comes to Chelo waiting on a dark patio of the restaurant. There is one candle lit in a bottle.)

CHELO: Ay Pipo. What are you doing wandering around alone? Where's your mother?

PIPO: She deserted me.

CHELO: No, she hasn't. She'll be back. Don't cry. I'll take care of you as long as you want. Hush. Hush.

PIPO: She'll die without me. She always told me so.

CHELO: Was she hurt then? Where did you last see her?

PIPO: On the bridge. When the man with the hat came. He took her away. I heard her cry out.

CHELO: The hat?

PIPO: The hat and the horse of bones. I forget his name.

CHELO: Ay—my little boy.

PIPO: What shall we do?

CHELO: Wait.

PIPO: Shhhh.

CHELO: What do you hear?

PIPO: The wind.

CHELO: I'll sing to you—so you won't hear. Come here. *(She sits and holds him.)*

Ay de mi Llorona, Llorona
Llorona a field of flowers
Ay de mi Llorona, Llorona
Llorona a field of flowers
If you've never really loved, Llorona
You don't know pain and sorrow
If you've never really loved, Llorona
You don't know pain and sorrow

SCENE 9

The next morning by the river Mundo is bathing. We see his upper body through leaves.

MUNDO: *(Singing overlapping with Chelo first and then continuing.)*
Ay de me Llorona Llorona
Llorona take me to the river
Ay de mi Llorona Llorona
Llorona take me to the river
Wrap me in your shawl, Llorona
The wind is cold as winter
Wrap me in your shawl, Llorona
The wind is cold as winter
(He hums a bit. He looks at his arms.)
Not cold. No.
(He washes himself, he touches his skin.)
A tree. Bark.
(He starts scrubbing hard, then harder trying to make his skin smooth.)
Off.
(He looks closely to see if he has an effect. He touches his arm and then puts his fingers to his mouth. He pats his arm. He's bleeding.)
Blood.

SCENE 10

Alicia comes to find Eddie.

ALICIA: Eddie?
EDDIE: Shhhh. Can you hear Mundo's singing?
(They both listen.)
ALICIA: He stopped.
EDDIE: You all right?
ALICIA: And you?
EDDIE: Come here.
(She doesn't.)
ALICIA: What happened with Nyin?

EDDIE: Nothing much.

ALICIA: He was furious.

EDDIE: I guess the truth makes him furious.

ALICIA: You shouldn't have said anything.

EDDIE: He shouldn't have messed with me.

ALICIA: Nyin might leave because of this. They've been together for thirty years!

EDDIE: Hey! Are you blaming me? I didn't betray Nyin.

ALICIA: You betrayed Chelo.

EDDIE: What is this? I did it for "us", all right? I don't want to lose you. They've got their own problems to solve. Maybe we can solve some of our own.

ALICIA: If you were angry at me, would you betray me too?

EDDIE: Of course not.

ALICIA: How do you know?

EDDIE: Alicia what can I tell you. What I do now is all I have. I could die tomorrow.

(A loud splash. A cry. The goat bleats.)

EDDIE: What's that?

ALICIA: Mundo—shame on you. Are you spying on us? *(To Eddie.)* Go see what he's doing.

EDDIE: *(Goes to the edge of the stage.)* It is Mundo. He's slipped. *(He holds out his hand and walks offstage.)* Here. Take my hand you idiot. Don't be stubborn! *(Eddie exits.)*

ALICIA: *(watches)* Eddie! Grab him. What's the matter? Eddie!

EDDIE: A branch. Get me a branch. *(Enters wet and muddy.)* Oh my God Alicia. He's gone. He wouldn't take my hand. He wouldn't take it.

ALICIA: *(Starts to run offstage.)* Mundo. Mundo.

EDDIE: You can't go in. There's a shark.

ALICIA: It's your fault. You talked about death.

EDDIE: Don't be stupid Alicia. Just saying a word doesn't call down the wrath of God. I held out my hand, but he backed away from me.

SCENE 11

At Chelo's restaurant patio. Chelo is sweeping. The boy Pipo is helping her. The Woman with Blue Eyes walks in.

PIPO: Oh, Mama. You didn't leave me!

WOMAN: What a stupid boy. How could I leave you? You're my son. *(She hugs him.)* Bobo. Frightened at every little thing.

CHELO: Where are you going? Your work's finished. Pack your things. Take some food from the kitchen and a beer. There's no place for you here.

(Nyin enters.)

WOMAN: You promised me two months work!

CHELO: I don't remember.

WOMAN: *(Imploring to Nyin.)* And you...you there—what do you say?

CHELO: Yes, what do you say?

NYIN: I have nothing to say about this. This isn't my decision.

CHELO: No?

NYIN: No.

CHELO: I think this may be the most important decision you've made in your life. The Woman with Blue Eyes says I promised her two months work. But I'm telling her I don't remember and I want her to leave now. So what do you say, Nyin. I need to know.

WOMAN: Well...husband?

NYIN: *(Bows his head. To Chelo.)* Fire her!

WOMAN: I see. All your talk of freedom for nothing. You might as well be married you two. You're acting like all men and their wives. Not a human heart between you. You both've used me and now it's out—eh? Well, I wouldn't stay anyway! Not me! Too much time in one place makes me itchy. Come on boy, we've learned our lesson here.

CHELO: You can leave the boy. You're always complaining about him anyway.

WOMAN: Would you like that? School? Other children? Meals till you burst?

PIPO: *(Holding her.)* Yes, Mama. Please.

WOMAN: No, you can't have him. I need him...What would I be without him? Let's go.

PIPO: The air's green and the wind might get us on the road. Where will we go?

WOMAN: What do you care? Come on!

(They exit.)

SCENE 12

Later that morning. We hear thunder. Chelo's restaurant patio. Eddie and Alicia enter.

EDDIE: Chelo? Chelo?
(Alicia sits heavily at one of the tables.)
EDDIE: I'll go look inside? Okay?
(Alicia says nothing.)
EDDIE: Do you want something…coffee maybe?
ALICIA: No.
(Eddie goes offstage and returns with a sweater.)
EDDIE: *(He goes to put it around Alicia's shoulders.)* Here.
ALICIA: I don't need it.
EDDIE: Okay. No one's around. *(He sits and then gets up immediately and paces.)* Pride killed him. Not me. Not me. I gave him my hand.
ALICIA: Maybe he wanted to die.
EDDIE: No. He stood up. He crossed his arms and looked at me. He never saw the sharks.
ALICIA: How like a man—not to back down, even when every leaf, every stone around him all but screams that he should. Machismo!
EDDIE: Why are you looking at me?
(Nyin and Chelo enter dressed up.)
ALICIA: Can you admit when you're wrong?
EDDIE: Aunt Chelo—
CHELO: *(Ignoring him. To no one in particular.)* We've been to church.
NYIN: Last night the devil made his rounds. One night changed my life. Who am I to fight it?
CHELO: He's been to confession.
EDDIE: Uncle Nyin…
CHELO: You're not welcome here.
ALICIA: Doña Chelo! Mundo drowned.
CHELO: Ay no! May God rest his soul.
NYIN: Poor thing.
CHELO: What happened?
ALICIA: He's dead.
NYIN: *(To Eddie.)* High tide?
EDDIE: High tide.
CHELO: Poor sad thing. May he rest in peace.

NYIN: I'll take my boat and see if he was carried downstream.

EDDIE: There were sharks.

NYIN: If he's anywhere—he'll be at the river's mouth. Poor thing.

CHELO: Be careful, Nyin.

NYIN: I tell you, the Devil made his rounds last night.

ALICIA: He was so lonely.

NYIN: Maybe it was for the best. What future did he have? Creature like that. A man isn't meant to live so alone.

(Nyin exits.)

CHELO: He had a voice of an angel.

ALICIA: *(To Nyin.)* Bring his goat. He's tied by the river.

(Nyin exits.)

EDDIE: Auntie—

CHELO: We'll talk.

EDDIE: It's too new. It's too deep. I can't be away from her now. Auntie. Listen to me.

(Chelo avoids him.)

EDDIE: I'd do anything for Alicia. I'd do what I've already done all over again—and more! I'd lie for her. I'd die for her. I'd take the clothes off your back for her and leave you shivering. And if that makes me like my father, that's too damn bad.

CHELO: Ay Edmundo—don't you know yet? You're nothing like your father.

EDDIE: What do you mean?

CHELO: Your father loves no one but himself.

EDDIE: I'll marry her.

ALICIA: And what am I—a bag of beans you two are tossing around? I have my thoughts about this. Edmundo doesn't belong here. I don't want him. Mundo knew too. He wouldn't take Eddie's hand to save his life. He wouldn't owe his life to a stranger and neither will I!

EDDIE: How can you say I'm a stranger?

ALICIA: I look at you now and you're a complete stranger. A month ago, you didn't exist. A month from now you won't either.

EDDIE: You don't mean that. You're upset…

ALICIA: The first person you saw in Nautla was Mundo. Now he's dead.

EDDIE: So what's that supposed to mean?

ALICIA: You're released. You're free to go. God wants you to leave.

EDDIE: God wants me to leave?

ALICIA: It's a sign. I'm sure.

EDDIE: You bitch. Don't use God as an excuse to blow me off. Just admit it—you don't want me around. Go ahead. Now that you have a choice—all you wanted was a little taste of foreign fruit—right? Go on—admit it.

ALICIA: You're right. That's all I wanted.

EDDIE: No, Alicia.

(Alicia exits.)

EDDIE: My father said women were treacherous bitches—maybe he was right!

CHELO: Edmundo…Edmundo.

EDDIE: What?

CHELO: Men are so blind.

EDDIE: What!

CHELO: She's making it easy for you. To leave. That's what women do best. Now go get Mundo's goat.

SCENE 13

Eddie looking for the goat. Thunder.

EDDIE: Come here. Come here. How the hell do you call a goat? Here boy…Here…*(He finds Mundo's pail and pole. He hits the pail and waits. He tries again and waits. He sings quietly.)*
I carry two kisses always, Llorona
very close to my soul
I carry two kisses always, Llorona
very close to my soul
The last one my mother gave me, Llorona
And the first kiss of yours I stole
The last one my mother gave me, Llorona
And the first kiss…

(We hear the bleating of a goat.) There you are little guy. Over here…
(He exits.)

SCENE 14

In church. Nyin and Chelo are kneeling. Alicia and Eddie slip the marriage lazo over their heads and go kneel in a pew.

ALICIA: Edmundo, Eddie—the priest told me—if you're ever in church and you can't pray—you should ask God to join your thoughts to the good prayers of the people around you.

EDDIE: Like you?

ALICIA: Yes.

EDDIE: Thanks.

ALICIA: Eddie?

EDDIE: Shhh. I'm praying.

ALICIA: Leave. Go. But don't forget me.

SCENE 15

Eddie reading a poem to an audience.

EDDIE: This poem is called "Plane Ride Home" for obvious reasons.
Leaving Mexico behind,
letting it sink into the sea
while the great continents come
unmoored as they pass my window
stirring the ocean into flowers of
foam and widening their arms into
peninsulas; I leave forever,
foundering on the tusks of
a thousand green volcanoes;
memories
streaming from me like rain;
the bells of churches
echoing in my throat.
I am scattered
Blown north, south
into mystery like the unglimpsed
Peak of Orizaba mist-hung

in July. Summer guardian
you've betrayed me into carrying you
away with me. Wedge against my rib, are
you sword or are you shield?

END OF PLAY

CLASS ACTION
by Brad Slaight

BIOGRAPHY

Brad Slaight is a Los Angeles–based actor-comic-writer. He has been on staff and written jokes and sketch material for numerous television shows and radio programs including: "The Tonight Show" (NBC); "The Sunday Comics" (FOX); "Into The Night" (ABC); "Evening at the Improv" (A&E); "Haywire!" (FOX); Cutler Radio Network (SYNDICATED), as well as a script for the sit-com "Just the Ten of Us" (ABC). Recently *National Lampoon* contracted Brad to create special comedy material for a CD-Rom computer program. He has also written several stage plays, including *Sightings* and *High Tide*. In addition to writing, Brad is a popular actor and stand-up comic who works extensively on TV and in clubs throughout the country. His many television and film credits include "The Young and the Restless," "Married, with Children," "Unsolved Mysteries," and "Freshman Dorm." He was recently voted "Comedian of the Year" by *Playboy*.

AUTHOR'S NOTE

The many scenes in *Class Action* collectively make up the "play." Although each scene stands on its own, there is a common thread here: All the scenes deal with situations that take place outside the classroom. It is my opinion that these events are sometimes the most important experiences that young people deal with in high school.

Brad Slaight

ORIGINAL PRODUCTION

Class Action was written for and first produced by the Young Conservatory at the American Conservatory Theater (Carey Perloff, Artistic Director; Craig Slaight, Young Conservatory Director), San Francisco, California, in May 1994. Directed by Amy Mueller; Assistant Director/Piano Accompaniment by Nick Edwards; Lighting Design by Kelly Roberson. The ensemble cast was as follows:

Kierstin Barile
Danton Char

Samer Danfoura
Natalie Lee
Sarah Palmer
Maria Sideris
Richard Tayloe

The playwright wishes to thank Craig Slaight and Amy Mueller for their invaluable guidance and suggestions.

CHARACTERS
seven students: four women, three men
Depending on your casting needs, and since there are many scenes and characters, you may choose to use more or less than the suggested cast.

TIME
The present.

SETTING
A modern high school. An open playing area containing several boxes and benches, which can be used as suggestive set pieces.

COSTUMES
Basic school clothes and suggestive props (glasses, hats, and so forth).

CLASS ACTION

SCENE 1

The cast is onstage as the audience enters. It should appear that they are in class and reading out of textbooks, or writing. When it's time to start the show, a bell is heard. The cast will begin to disperse and talk among themselves, as if class has been dismissed. The house lights fade, as the stage lights come up. Beth and Lisa enter from opposite sides and meet in the middle of the stage.

BETH: Lisa!

LISA: Beth!

BETH: News?

LISA: Nothing.

BETH: Carl?

LISA: No!

BETH: David?

LISA: David!

BETH: Date?

LISA: Called.

BETH: Really?

LISA: Really.

BETH: And?

LISA: Possible.
BETH: Lucky.
LISA: Hopeful.
BETH: Parents?
LISA: Clue-less.
BETH: Risky.
LISA: Right.
BETH: When?
LISA: Saturday.
BETH: Where?
LISA: Mall.
BETH: Sneaky.
LISA: Genius.
BETH: Happy?
LISA: You?
BETH: Brad.
LISA: Double?
BETH: Maybe.
LISA: Party.
BETH: Brad?
LISA: Right.
BETH: Embarrassing.
LISA: Sorry.
BETH: Tommy.
LISA: Tommy?
BETH: Hoping.
LISA: Good.
   (A bell is heard.)
LISA: Damn.
BETH: Already.
LISA: Algebra.
BETH: Choir.
LISA: Lucky.
BETH: 'Bye.
LISA: Later.
   (They both exit.)

SCENE 2

Karen and Leon sit in desks, back-to-back; nothing is said for a few moments.

LEON: What time is it now?

KAREN: Two minutes later than the last time you asked.

LEON: Oh, yeah. *(long pause)* I've never been in detention before.

KAREN: You already told me that.

LEON: Oh, yeah.

KAREN: But you didn't tell me why you're here.

LEON: Is it important?

KAREN: You're doin' time...let's hear the crime.

LEON: I pulled the fire alarm Tuesday.

KAREN: *(impressed)* That was you?

LEON: That was me.

KAREN: A guy like you...I'll bet you thought there really was a fire.

LEON: No, I knew there wasn't.

KAREN: Well, well...Little Leon Mosher has a bad side to him. Why did you do it? Were you pissed at a teacher? Stressed out by the system?

LEON: Well, uh...none of the above.

KAREN: This ain't a multiple-choice test, Mosher. If it wasn't one of those reasons, why'd you do it?

LEON: You'll just laugh at me.

KAREN: Probably, but give it a shot.

LEON: I did it so I could get a chance to be with you.

(Karen stares at him for a moment.)

LEON: You're not laughing.

KAREN: You're right.

LEON: You see, I always wanted to talk to you, away from the crowd you hang with...Ever since we were kids, but you're never alone.

KAREN: So I have a lot of friends, you got a problem with that?

LEON: I know you're different when you're away from the others. You pretend to be so tough and everything, but I know you're not like that.

KAREN: Is that right?

LEON: I may seem like a real dork to you, but one thing I pride myself on is that I know people. I can see through the fake sincerity of Sue Powell our Homecoming Queen, and I can also see the beautiful person beneath your tough talk and ever present scowl. And I mean that as a compliment.

(She turns around and stares at him for a moment.)

KAREN: Let me get this straight...You got yourself two weeks of detention just to be with me?

LEON: Yes. *(long pause)* I wanted to ask you out on a date. Nothing major, just a coke or something. Like, maybe after detention today?

KAREN: A date? Just you and me?

LEON: That's what I was hoping for.

KAREN: Alright, Leon, but just one coke. Only because you pulled the alarm, and I like stuff like that.

LEON: Without all your friends?

KAREN: Like I'd want them to know.

LEON: You got a point there. *(long pause)* What time is it now?

KAREN: Don't push your luck, Leon.

LEON: Oh, yeah.

SCENE 3

Andrea paces, while Nina sits writing on a yellow notepad.

ANDREA: What do we have so far?

NINA: Just the title.

ANDREA: We've been working on this stupid story for over two hours and all we have is a title?

NINA: And even that sucks.

ANDREA: I kinda like it.

NINA: "The Perfect Guy?"

ANDREA: It's got a certain mystery about it.

NINA: Yeah, the mystery is we're never gonna finish this story. It's due tomorrow.

ANDREA: Alright, let's quit arguing and start writing.

NINA: How about this? *(She writes.)* "It was a dark stormy night when I heard the knock at my door."

(We hear a knock.)

NINA: "A stranger walked in...he had a hunchback and limped badly."

(One of the male players limps in, wearing a hump.)

ANDREA: No way. Not a hunchback. Make him more romantic.

(Nina scratches off part of what she has written, the Hunchback exits.)

NINA: "A stranger walked in, he was a young handsome man…"

ANDREA: With a thick English accent!

(Another male player enters.)

YOUNG MAN: *(thick English accent)* Pardon me, mates…I've had a bit of an accident with my jalopy and I need to call a bobby.

NINA: I hate foreign accents. *(writes)* "He was a well spoken guy from the Midwest."

YOUNG MAN: Excuse me, ladies…My Camaro threw a rod and I gotta call Triple A.

ANDREA: I want an English guy.

NINA: You should have thought about that before you made me do all the writing.

ANDREA: Alright, so he needs to use the phone. Uh…oh, I know. The phone is out because of the storm.

NINA: Good. "Suddenly the power goes out."

(Lights flicker; then fade, but not all the way.)

ANDREA: Just because the power goes out, doesn't mean the phone is dead.

NINA: Oh yeah, watch this. "He crosses to the phone and picks it up, but…"

YOUNG MAN: Phone's dead. Must be because of the storm.

ANDREA: I don't know…

NINA: Trust me, Andrea, it works.

ANDREA: So then he decides that he has to stay the night with us.

NINA: *(writes)* "He turns and faces the two girls."

YOUNG MAN: Look, do you think I could stay here for the night?

ANDREA: This is getting interesting…How about, "The two girls light some candles and get to know him better."

NINA: I got a better idea. *(writes)* "Realizing he will be staying the night, he looks at the two girls more closely. He crosses to Andrea…"

(The young man crosses to Andrea, she flirts with him with her eyes.)

NINA: "A nice girl, but rather plain, he thinks to himself."

ANDREA: Hey!

NINA: "He then casts his eyes on Nina, drinking her vision, dazzled by her beauty. Crosses to her and reaches for her hand."

(The young man crosses to Nina, takes her hand and kisses it gently.)

YOUNG MAN: "You are totally beautiful."

ANDREA: Nina, this is supposed to be our story. And besides he's a Perfect Guy, not *your* perfect guy.

(Nina continues to write frantically.)

NINA: "He is so overcome with Nina that he sweeps her up in his arms...

(He picks her up.)

NINA: "And carries her out of the room, down the hall, where they kiss passionately for the rest of the stormy evening!"

(They start to exit, Nina tears the pages off the note pad and discards the unused portion to the floor as they leave.)

ANDREA: Nina, wait...what about the assignment? Nina! *(Andrea picks up the note pad.)* Alright, I'll just write the story myself and you can flunk. *(She pauses to think, then starts to write.)* "It was late fall when Andrea's boyfriend from *England* came to visit."

(We hear a knock on the door; she opens it and another actor enters.)

ANDREA: *(writing)* "She was a little mad at him for being late, but when he showed her the roses, she smiled and forgave him."

(He holds up a dozen roses, previously hidden behind his back.)

ENGLISH YOUNG MAN: *(with accent)* "Lovely to see you, my little bird."

ANDREA: "This was going to be a night that they would both remember for a long, long time...

SCENE 4

Danielle enters, she places her hand on her womb area.

DANIELLE: I haven't started to show yet, so most everyone thinks that I'm moody because I broke up with Richie. That's partly true, although I don't blame him for not wanting the burden of having this kid. We're both only seventeen. He wanted me to "take care of it", and even though I believe in the whole choice thing, my choice was to keep her. Oh, I know it will be a "girl" because I'm hardly sick or anything, and my Aunt Susan told me that it's always baby boys that make a pregnant woman nauseous. She should know...she had four. My Aunt Susan's been real cool about this. I told her before I told anybody, because we've always had a special friendship. Richie doesn't talk to me much anymore, and I'm sure some of my friends are going to be pretty weird around me when I start swelling. But somehow none of that seems to matter. I know that I'll be able to handle all the problems that come along because there is someone who is much more important than all of them put together. And she is inside me now. Waiting to help me. Waiting to need me.

SCENE 5

Jack, a jock type, sits and writes in a notebook; hides it when he sees Joni.

JONI: I saw you writing in your notebook, you can't fool me.

JACK: Hi, Joni.

JONI: You haven't finished your English assignment, have you?

JACK: Uh…not really.

JONI: I know you so well, Jack Heller.

JACK: Yeah…

JONI: You always wait until the last minute.

JACK: What were we s'pose to do?

JONI: Poetry! Remember, we have to turn in a poem? Mrs. Vernon only told us five or six times.

JACK: Guess my head was somewhere else.

JONI: Want to hear mine?

JACK: Sure.

(Joni takes a paper out and reads from it proudly.)

JONI: "Love…by Joni Mendez:

I was riding in my car,

I was riding all alone

I was riding in my car

Going through the radar zone.

The policeman clocked my speed,

At 80 miles per hour

He asked me why I sped like that

Calling me a wild flower.

So I told him that I hadn't seen

My guy for over a week

And I was rushing to see him

So the two of us could speak.
The cop he smiled and said okay
He understood my longing heart.
And let me continue on my way.
So my love and me would no longer be apart.

JACK: Wow…that's great.

JONI: I guess I just have a way with words.

JACK: Wish I could write like that.

JONI: You just concentrate on winning the game tonight. I've already taken care of your assignment…I wrote your poem for you, so you can stop worrying.

JACK: Really?

(She holds up paper.)

JONI: It's called "Broken Heart" and it's almost as good as the one I wrote for myself. I better hold it for you until class, you'll probably lose it.
(She kisses him on the cheek, and then exits. Jack makes sure she is gone; opens his notebook back up and reads from it.)

JACK: "Winterscape. A Poem by Jack Heller"
A vibrant glaze slips upon the busy hillside
Blowing a blue chill like notes from
An angry saxophone
Upon the unsuspecting hollow heart world
Hunkering down the brown leaf child of fall
And causing a pond frog to scream
His protest at the dormant mud.
And with a simple dark shade
Closes the lid
Closes the winterscape
Closes the world
For now.

(Jack tears the poem from his notebook; shoves it in his back pocket. Picks up his notebook and spins his football in the air as he exits.)

SCENE 6

Tina and Robby sit close together, as if they were parked in a car. Their position is romantic, but their expressions are not.

TINA: Haven't we been here long enough?

ROBBY: I say we give it another five minutes. *(pause)* Look who just pulled up...

TINA: That surprises you? Gale and Lyle come here to make out all the time.

ROBBY: I know...I just thought that tonight maybe they'd get a motel room or somethin'.

(pause)

TINA: This dress has some kind of wires in the bra...it's starting to cut into my skin.

ROBBY: Yeah, well this tuxedo sucks. I told the guy the cumberbum was too small.

TINA: Cummerbund...it's called a cummerbund.

ROBBY: Whatever...it's too small.

TINA: Just take it off.

ROBBY: Hey, with what I paid for it, I'm gonna wear it until I take it back.

(Tina nudges him and nods toward another part of the stage.)

TINA: Look, Susie and Tom are doin' it.

ROBBY: How can you tell?

TINA: The fact that their car is rocking back and forth is a pretty good clue.

ROBBY: Think we should get this thing rockin', too?

(She gives him a look.)

ROBBY: I didn't mean for real, I meant pretend...like we've been doin' all night.

TINA: Nah, people would really get suspicious then. We've never even dated before.

ROBBY: I don't see why we have to pretend at all. Why don't we just tell everyone that we didn't want to go to the prom alone, so we decided to go together?

TINA: Because that makes us look like a couple of losers.

ROBBY: We are a couple of losers.

TINA: Speak for yourself.

(Pause; suddenly Robby pulls her in tight.)

TINA: What are you doing?

ROBBY: Karla and Jonathan are just two cars away…they can see us.

TINA: So?

ROBBY: So, I asked Karla to go to the prom with me and she turned me down. I don't want her to think we're just sittin' up here.

TINA: She turned you down? Who does she think she is?

ROBBY: Yeah, right. Who does she think she is? (pause) Man, I feel so stupid.

TINA: How do you think I feel?

ROBBY: Hey, you could have at least gone with another girl. Lots of 'em paired off. But if I went with a buddy, I'd be gay. Talk about your double standards.

(She nudges him again.)

TINA: Look, Connie and Tim are making out and this is only their second date.

ROBBY: Yeah, two weeks ago they didn't even know each other. (Robby looks at Tina for a moment.)

TINA: By the way, the corsage is very nice. I'll reimburse you for it tomorrow.

ROBBY: No hurry.

TINA: Minus what I paid for your boutonniere.

ROBBY: My what?

TINA: The flower I gave you.

ROBBY: Oh, right. (pause) Uh…maybe we should, you know…you know.

TINA: No I don't know. Maybe we should what?

ROBBY: Well, if anyone is lookin' at us, like we're lookin' at them…I thought maybe we should kiss or something.

TINA: I don't know?

ROBBY: Only a pretend kiss.

TINA: You may be right…it would certainly remove any doubt, in case we are being watched.

ROBBY: Alright, go ahead.

TINA: You're the guy, you're supposed to be the kisser…I'm the kissee.

ROBBY: Right. (Robby awkwardly puts his arm around her; gives her a quick peck on the lips.)

TINA: I get more romantic kisses from my little brother. If you're going to do it…do it right.

(Robby hesitates, then really lays one on her. It is a long, compassionate kiss. When they come up for air, they've both been affected by it.)

TINA: (overwhelmed) That was better.

ROBBY: *(also affected)* Yeah.

    (pause)

TINA: Look, there's Melanie...maybe we should kiss again so...

    (Before she can finish her sentence, Robby kisses her again. Even longer than before. Finally they pull away from each other and recover.)

ROBBY: *(looking at watch)* Well, I think it would be okay if we left now.

TINA: We've certainly proved our point.

ROBBY: Yes we have. *(Robby reaches to start the car.)*

TINA: You start that car and you're a dead man! *(Tina pulls him in for another kiss.)*

SCENE 7

Nate enters, bouncing a basketball.

NATE: He shoots, he scores! *(He makes a sound of fans cheering.)* The excitement of the game is everything to me. I think it went back to when I was three and my Uncle Joey gave me a Fisher-Price toy hoop and ball. My Mom says I wouldn't play with any of my other toys after that. It was throw the ball in the hoop, pick up the ball, throw the ball in the hoop, pick up the ball...all day long. When I was ten, my Dad put a backboard and hoop up over the garage. I made him make it regulation, even though it was way too high for me. I only made maybe one in ten shots. But I practiced every day, and dreamed about basketball every night. I sat on the bench most of Junior High, holding onto the hope that I would soon grow and I could be a first stringer. But I didn't grow. My Doctor says I'm a late bloomer, it may not even happen until I'm eighteen or nineteen. Great. So, since our school doesn't have a horse racing team in need of a jockey, and since I'm still addicted to basketball, I signed on as the team's Manager. Hey, it's not so bad. I still get the best seat at all the games. I still get to be in the team picture. And I still get to be around basketball. The excitement of the game is everything to me.

SCENE 8

Laura sits at a library study table. Melanie and Janine enter and sit next to her. Other students people the scene and will "shush" occasionally when the conversations get too loud. Mike enters and notices Laura with her friends, decides to sit with Scooter at a nearby table.

MELANIE: I can't believe the cafeteria served mystery meat three days in a row. Wonder what we ate today?

LAURA: I think it was pork.

JANINE: It might have just been bad chicken.

MELANIE: Eee-yo. *(Melanie looks at Janine.)*

JANINE: You know, I heard the weirdest rumor about you, Laura.

MELANIE: I heard it, too.

LAURA: Really?

JANINE: Somebody said they saw you out on a date last night with that fat kid Mike Howard. *(Janine notices Mike.)* Oh God, he's sitting right over there.

(Laura reacts.)

MELANIE: We told them that you were both in the school play and were probably just practicing your lines.

JANINE: That had to be it, right?

(They both wait for Laura to respond.)

LAURA: We are both in the school play.

MELANIE: *(relieved)* See, I knew there was a good reason.

LAURA: And we also went out on a date.

(Crosscut to Mike and Scooter, who whisper at a nearby table.)

SCOOTER: I tell you you're the King of the Misfits. You've given every nerd in this school a reason to live.

MIKE: Is that supposed to be a compliment?

SCOOTER: Laura Rivers…you captured the crown jewels, baby.

STUDENT: Ssshhhh!

MIKE: You make it sound like a sport.

SCOOTER: Don't kid yourself, dating is a sport. And you just won the Superbowl.

MIKE: I don't appreciate you making Laura sound like some kind of trophy.

SCOOTER: That's good. Sticking up for your woman is what you should be doin'.

MIKE: She's not my woman.

SCOOTER: You went out with her, didn't you?

MIKE: We went to a movie together. That's all.

SCOOTER: That's all? You make it sound like she'd go to a movie with just anybody.

(Back to Laura, Melanie, and Janine.)

JANINE: The two of you have nothing in common: You're a Senior, he's a Junior; you're popular, he's in the loser patrol; you're gorgeous, he's fat.

MELANIE: People are talking. They're calling you two "Beauty and the Beef".

LAURA: And of course you defended me because I'm your friend?

JANINE: Yes, we told them that you just feel sorry for him.

MELANIE: Because that is why you went out with him, isn't it?

LAURA: I went out with Mike Howard because he's talented, sincere, and has a great sense of humor.

JANINE: You could have your pick of any guy in this school.

LAURA: He's really sweet. You don't know him…

MELANIE: We don't want to know him.

JANINE: Right.

LAURA: He's very special to me.

JANINE: Special enough to ruin your whole life? Because that's what's going to happen if you keep on dating him.

LAURA: Ruin my life?

MELANIE: He's just using you, Laura. To make himself look good.

(Back to Mike and Scooter.)

MIKE: Laura is very sweet.

SCOOTER: She's been on the cover of a magazine…she's a model. Models aren't sweet…they're sexy, they're dangerous, they're nasty.

MIKE: It's not like that with us.

SCOOTER: Ah-hah, you used the "us" word. This is serious.

MIKE: We're just friends.

SCOOTER: No, you and I are friends. You and Laura are lovers.

MIKE: Yeah, right.

SCOOTER: The whole school is talkin' about it.

MIKE: Yeah, I heard…"Beauty and the Beef"

(Back to Laura, Melanie, and Janine.)

LAURA: It's bad enough that I have to get my parents' approval when I date, I shouldn't have to get my friends'.

JANINE: It's because we're friends that we're telling you this.

MELANIE: We don't want to see you get hurt.

LAURA: Jeff hurt me, Rick hurt me…Mike Howard is the first guy I've ever gone out with that actually cares about how *I* feel.

MELANIE: If he really cares about you, he'll realize that he's wrong for you.

JANINE: Dating a guy like that can give you a bad reputation. People judge you by who you're with.

LAURA: Like when I hang out with you two?

JANINE: You know what I mean.

LAURA: So I go out on a date with someone and if others don't approve then I run the risk of losing my social position here at school?

MELANIE: You say it like you don't think it matters, but you know it does.

JANINE: This is the most important time of your life, don't screw it up.

MELANIE: We're only trying to help you.

(Back to Scooter and Mike.)

SCOOTER: They wouldn't talk if something' wasn't going on. And something is going on, isn't it?

MIKE: Why are you pressuring me about this?

SCOOTER: Why are you avoiding the obvious?

MIKE: I don't want to push it, okay. She's the first girl who ever paid any attention to me…and I like that.

SCOOTER: I think you can get more than attention from her.

MIKE: Right now I enjoy being with her. If I push things, I may ruin it. I may not have her love, but I have *her*. And I don't want to risk losing that.

SCOOTER: That's poetic, but it just doesn't work that way.

(Back to Laura, Melanie, and Janine.)

JANINE: Look, there's a party over at Kelly's house this weekend. I know for a fact that Martin Dole has been asking about you ever since you broke up with Rick. This would be the perfect time for the two of you to talk…

MELANIE: It's going to be the party of the year. Everybody will be there, it'll be the perfect time to let people know that you're…you know…

(They both look at Laura, waiting for an answer.)

LAURA: Alright, I'll go to the party.

(They are relieved.)

MELANIE: You've made the right decision.

JANINE: You really had us worried.

LAURA: What time should Mike and I be there? *(Laura gets up and heads over to Mike.)*

(Back to Mike and Scooter.)

SCOOTER: If you don't make a play for Laura soon, she's going shopping…and I don't mean for clothes.

(Mike gets up and starts to leave.)

SCOOTER: It's time you stop thinking with your head, and start thinking with your penis!

(Everyone in the library hears that. Laura reaches an embarrassed Mike and they exit together.)

SCENE 9
Dennis enters.

DENNIS: My name is Dennis Gandleman. Around this school I am the object of ridicule from most of the students, simply because I have an extremely high I.Q. It's 176. My father wanted me to enroll in a special school that deals with geniuses like myself, but Mother was firmly against that. She wanted me to have a normal education, and not be treated as some kind of freak…Which is ironic, because that's exactly what is happening to me here. The whole concept of education is a paradox: High School is supposed to celebrate education and knowledge, but what it really celebrates is social groups and popularity. In a perfect world, a kid like me would be worshiped because of my scholastic abilities, instead of someone who can throw a 40-yard touchdown pass. I suppose I could complain, and bemoan the unfairness of it all. But I am bright. I know something that the others don't…That, once we leave High School and enter the real world, all the rules change. What matters is power. Financial power. Power that comes from making a fortune on cutting edge computer software. Software that I am already developing. *(pause)* Some call me a nerd. I call myself…ahead of my time. See you on the outside.

SCENE 10

Jonathan enters and spots Karla; at the same time two other players, boy and girl enter. They stand on boxes behind Jonathan and Karla acting as their "subtext."

JONATHAN: Hi Karla.

BOY: I hope she didn't find out about last night.

KARLA: *(cold)* Jonathan.

GIRL: You jerk.

JONATHAN: So, we still on for tonight?

BOY: I bet that big mouth Angela told her.

KARLA: That depends if you can work me into your schedule.

GIRL: How could you do this to me?

JONATHAN: You sound upset, what's goin' on?

BOY: Maybe if I just play dumb she'll drop it.

KARLA: Don't play dumb with me.

GIRL: Although for you it's very easy.

JONATHAN: Is this about me going to the Mall with Lisa?

BOY: Or was it Julie and the movies?

KARLA: You know darn well that's what I'm talking about.

GIRL: Let's see you get out of this one.

JONATHAN: I was looking for a birthday gift for you, she was helping me
    pick out something nice.

BOY: She's not buying it.

KARLA: Yeah, right.

GIRL: I'm not buying it.

JONATHAN: Why do you always have to be so jealous?

BOY: Why can't you just let me use you?

GIRL: That's the problem with you, you use everyone you date.

BOY: Yeah, well at least I pay for all the dates.

GIRL: You think money is everything.

BOY: Don't start with...

*(Boy and Girl stop arguing when they realize Karla and Jonathan are
staring at them; the scene continues.)*

KARLA: Why do you always have to lie to me?

GIRL: I'll make him feel guilty.

JONATHAN: We're dating, it's not like we're married or anything.

BOY: She's lucky to have me at all.

KARLA: Are you saying you want to break up?

GIRL: He thinks I'm kidding.

JONATHAN: Maybe we should.

BOY: I'm calling her bluff. Any minute now she'll start crying and apologizing and I'll pretend to be hurt that she doubted me.

KARLA: Fine, here's your ring back. It never fit right anyway.

GIRL: I should have done this months ago.

(She takes the ring off and throws it at him.)

JONATHAN: Wait a minute?

BOY: May day! May day! I'm going down. 911! 911!

KARLA: It's for the best, now we can both see whoever we want.

GIRL: Like Alan Meyers!

(Karla exits, and the girl subtext leaves with her.)

JONATHAN: Fine, it's better this way.

BOY: Don't just stand there, you idiot, go after her.

JONATHAN: Karla, wait…can't we talk about this?

(Jonathan and boy exit after her.)

BOY: I can't believe she dumped me.

SCENE 11

Arnold enters and stands on a chair, as if he is hiding. Bill enters and looks around.

BILL: I know you're in here, Arnold. So don't even try to hide from me.

(Arnold stays frozen. Bill moves down the line, looking under each imaginary bathroom stall.)

BILL: This is like a freakin' game show. Are you behind door #1? Door #2…(He suddenly skips door #3 and goes right to where Arnold is.) …or door #4? (opens imaginary door) Out…Now!

(Arnold steps down; Bill grabs him by the shoulders and shoves him up against a wall.)

ARNOLD: Bill, wait…don't do it. I can explain. Just let me explain.

BILL: Make it quick, 'cause I'm kinda in a hurry and squashin' you is already cuttin' in to my fun time.

ARNOLD: I know you think I told Mrs. Pritchard that you cut out of class early when she wasn't looking, but I didn't say anything.

BILL: Then why did I hear it was you?

ARNOLD: I don't know. The only thing I can figure is that there's lots of kids in that class that don't like me. Especially after the last test when I threw off the curve by getting a perfect score while everyone else hit in the low 70s, but should I be penalized because I happen to study...

BILL: *(cutting him off)* Shut up. *(pause)* Man, no wonder everyone hates you.

ARNOLD: So you understand? Because that's how it happened. I was framed. I may be obnoxious, but I'm no tattletale.

BILL: Tattletale?

ARNOLD: It's a slang word for someone who squeals on someone else.

BILL: I know what it means, I just didn't think anyone over five still used the word.

ARNOLD: It wasn't me, I swear. You're about to squash an innocent man.

BILL: Even if I believed that, it makes no difference. Word's out that it was you, so if I don't waste you then it could hurt my rep. *(Bill draws his arm back.)*

ARNOLD: Oh, I get it. Big fish eats smaller fish.

BILL: Somethin' like that.

ARNOLD: Yeah, right. And beating somebody up is the way to settle the matter. I mean that's what your Father does to you, so naturally you have to do the same to me.

BILL: What are you talkin' about?

ARNOLD: Didn't think anybody knew, did you? Well I do. I know all about what goes on over at your house.

(Bill loosens his grip.)

ARNOLD: I spend a lot of time up on my roof at night looking through my telescope at the stars. Sometimes I get bored with the Big Dipper and aim my sights across the field to your house. Actually I feel sorry for you, and your Mother. The guy should be locked up, the way he treats you two.

(Bill lets go of Arnold. Arnold nervously awaits Bill's reaction.)

ARNOLD: I shouldn't have said that. But you had me cornered. I'm sorry. It's really none of my business.

(Pause; Bill takes a few steps away.)

BILL: He isn't always like that. But when he drinks he kinda loses it *(pause)* ...I don't let him go too far, and I *never* let him hurt Mom.

ARNOLD: Of course you don't.

BILL: My Dad hasn't worked for two years…two years! He keeps hopin'
they'll call him back, but I think he knows they never will.

ARNOLD: Look, just punch me out and get it over with? Forget I men-
tioned it.

BILL: But you did.

(Arnold steps toward him, but keeps a safe distance.)

ARNOLD: This may come as a surprise to you, but things aren't so great
at my place either. The reason I spend so much time on the roof isn't
because I'm that much into astronomy, it's that I'm that much into
staying away from my stepmother, or as I like to call her, my "step-
monster". My Dad has to work two jobs so she can sit home all day
and become a preferred customer on the Home Shopping Network.

BILL: Maybe you're right…maybe I was gonna hurt you because he hurt
me. I don't want that to be the reason, because that's not right.

ARNOLD: No, you were going to hurt me because you have your honor
to defend. Someone told you that I turned you in, you have no
choice but to seek your revenge. If word got out that you didn't re-
taliate…why everybody in school would start to challenge you. And
then what kind of social order would we have?

BILL: For bein' such a genius, you sure are actin' real stupid.

ARNOLD: You're right, I'm actually trying to talk you into beating me up.

(They both laugh at that; Bill starts to leave.)

ARNOLD: Where you going?

BILL: I'm gonna' take you on your word that you're not a tattle…that you
didn't turn me in.

ARNOLD: I didn't…I swear. *(beat)* But what about the others?

BILL: You let me worry about that.

ARNOLD: And you have my word that I'm not going to say anything
about what goes on over at your place.

BILL: Thanks. *(Bill starts to head out again.)*

ARNOLD: Bill, if you ever want to talk…You know, at night.

BILL: If I do, I'll look for ya up on your roof.

(Bill exits. Arnold breathes a sign of relief.)

SCENE 12

Emma enters alone.

EMMA: I screamed when the DJ told me I had not only won tickets to the concert, but backstage passes as well. *(She displays a backstage pass.)* I mean I had never won anything in my life, and then all of a sudden I was caller number twenty-five and on my way to the biggest concert of the year! The New Landlords were my favorite group, and the fact that I was going to get to meet them kept me from getting much sleep the rest of the week. The concert was everything I hoped it would be, I had the best seat in the house and my friend Cindy owed me big time for giving her the other ticket. She just about passed out when we went backstage to meet the band members. Eddie was my favorite and I almost fainted when they introduced him to me. He was the lead singer, and not really that much older than me, even though he looked like he was. Cindy was so caught up with all the excitement, she didn't see Eddie and me leave the party and go to his dressing room. *(pause)* I guess I should have known what was going on, but I honestly thought we were just going to get away from the noise and have a good talk. Eddie and me alone together, it was like a dream or something! His lyrics are so inspiring, so full of love that I was completely shocked when he pulled me over to a couch and started tearing at my clothes. Maybe if he would have kissed me or something first I wouldn't have reacted like I did, but he moved on me so quick. He got on top of me and started pulling at my shirt. He was much stronger than me and even though I pushed and told him no, he pinned me down. I started to panic because I felt trapped and he wouldn't listen to me. His rough beard was scratching my face. His breath made me nauseous. When he started to unzip his pants it gave me just enough room to swing my knee hard into his crotch, causing him to fall off me. I got out of there before he could go any further. *(pause)* I saw him on MTV the next week. He had makeup on, but I could still see the scratch marks where I gouged his face. I hope it never heals. *(She looks at the backstage pass and tosses it on the ground as she exits.)*

SCENE 13

Carmen and Joanne enter and cross down center.

CARMEN: You want to open her locker?

JOANNE: Not really. You do it.

> *(Carmen mimes opening a combination lock, then opens the locker. They stare inside for a moment.)*

CARMEN: This is so weird.

JOANNE: Really.

CARMEN: I feel like I'm breaking in, or something.

JOANNE: She was always pretty protective of her locker.

CARMEN: Better us than her parents. Or especially better than Vice Principal Adams.

> *(Joanne starts to remove items; places them in a box.)*

JOANNE: She didn't have anything bad in here, did she?

CARMEN: I don't think so, not after they raided her locker last semester.

JOANNE: Yeah, she got in major trouble even though all they found was an empty bottle.

CARMEN: I'm surprised they only found one.

JOANNE: You shouldn't say stuff like that, especially now.

CARMEN: Maybe if I'd have said stuff like that to her, she might still be alive.

JOANNE: My Mom said I was lucky that I wasn't riding in the car with her. Or I'd probably be dead too.

CARMEN: That sounds like a Mom thing to say. Mine wasn't much better. She asked me if I ever got drunk with Cindy.

JOANNE: What did you tell her?

CARMEN: I didn't answer. And she didn't push it.

> *(Joanne pulls out a small stuffed animal.)*

CARMEN: You gave her that for her birthday, didn't you?

JOANNE: Yeah.

CARMEN: You were the only one that gave her a present.

JOANNE: I can't believe her parents would forget something like that.

CARMEN: She told everyone that they were out of town.

JOANNE: Cindy was always covering for them.

CARMEN: You should keep it. It means something to you. She'd probably want you to have it.

> *(Joanne pulls out a small journal.)*

CARMEN: *(breaking a bit)* Cin's journal. She wrote in that every day. Remember what she called it?

JOANNE: "Shrink in a box". She always felt better after writing in it. *(pause)* She ever let you look at it?

CARMEN: Once. She just broke up with Jack and was pretty depressed. I asked her what was wrong and she just handed it to me to read.

JOANNE: Yeah. *(Joanne thumbs through it.)* There's something in here from Wednesday. The same day…

CARMEN: Let's not read it. Those were her private thoughts. It's not right that anybody reads it…especially her Mom.

JOANNE: But I told her we'd bring everything over to the house.

CARMEN: She'll never know.

JOANNE: I got an idea…let's slip it in her casket. You know, tonight at the Funeral Home, when no one is looking.

CARMEN: *(forcing a smile)* That's a real Cindy thing to do. She'd like that. *(pause)* We better go through all her papers and stuff. In case there's something else that Cindy wouldn't want her Mom to see.

JOANNE: Right. We can go over to my place first and sort through everything. *(Joanne removes a stack of books. Sad laugh.)* Look at these books, they're like new.

CARMEN: Cin never was much to study or anything.

JOANNE: This locker was so important to her.

CARMEN: It was her home base.

JOANNE: This makes everything so final. I really miss her.

CARMEN: Me, too.

JOANNE: The rest of this year is going to be pretty lame without her around.

CARMEN: Yeah.

JOANNE: It just won't be the same.

(A bell is heard.)

CARMEN: Let's get outta here before all the "looky loos" start hangin' around.

JOANNE: I've had enough of them.

(Carmen scoops the rest of the items into the box.)

JOANNE: Put the lock back on. I think it should stay empty the rest of the year.

CARMEN: I agree.

(Joanne picks up the box and starts to head off; Carmen puts the lock back on and pauses for a moment.)

JOANNE: Are you coming?

CARMEN: Yeah. *(Carmen places her open palm on the closed locker as a parting gesture and then exits with Joanne.)*

SCENE 14
Danny enters.

DANNY: Who would have ever thought that she would be mine? That I, Danny Logan, would ever have such a beauty all to myself. After looking at her for years, after wanting her for years, she is finally mine. And beautiful? When I'm with her, others turn their heads as we go by. It's her body. A perfect 10. She's older than me, but you'd never know it…and she's very powerful. What an incredible combination, beauty and power. It's a sign that I am no longer Danny Logan, the little kid next door, but Dan Logan, a man who has something that all other men only wish for. She is mine for now and forever. She has changed my life…A 1972 Camaro and she's all mine!

SCENE 15
Wanda sits wiping tears from her eyes, Tabitha enters and crosses to her.

TABITHA: I don't have to ask. It's pretty obvious you told Scott.

WANDA: Yes, I did.

TABITHA: How did he take it?

WANDA: A lot harder than I thought he would, that's why I'm so upset. I think I really hurt him.

TABITHA: Hey, don't feel guilty. He hurt you plenty of times.

WANDA: You're right. Just like you were right about me breaking up with him…I should have done it months ago.

TABITHA: He was using you.

WANDA: I know that. Well, not at first, but after you explained it to me…it really made things clear.

TABITHA: I didn't want to, but I figured since I was a friend it was my responsibility. I owed that to you.

WANDA: You're the best friend ever.

TABITHA: It just made me so mad how he would lie to you, cheat on you, and take you for granted.

WANDA: How could I have been so stupid not to see it myself?

TABITHA: Love does that to you, it gets in the way of things.

WANDA: It's like you said, I didn't really love Scott, I was just in love with the idea of being in love.

TABITHA: Exactly, even though you knew you were in a bad relationship, it was better than no relationship at all.

WANDA: I was.

TABITHA: You don't need him anymore.

WANDA: No, I don't. And that's exactly what I told him. "Scott, I don't need you anymore."

TABITHA: And he took it hard, huh?

WANDA: He was devastated. For a minute I almost changed my mind and took him back, but I kept remembering what you told me. That gave me strength.

TABITHA: If you would have folded, you would have been stuck with him for maybe the rest of your life.

WANDA: Scott is a jerk, and thank God you were there to point that out to me.

TABITHA: He's all looks and nothing else.

WANDA: A pretty package with no contents.

TABITHA: Nice building, no inventory.

WANDA: Good acting, bad script.

TABITHA: A limousine with a four cylinder engine.

(Wanda gives her a double take on that.)

TABITHA: So it's over for you two?

WANDA: Completely. It was a big scene. He screamed, I screamed. He cried, I cried. Everybody saw it.

TABITHA: That's good, then it makes it final.

WANDA: Very final.

(Scott approaches.)

TABITHA: Maybe not, here he comes now.

WANDA: Oh, no.

TABITHA: Be strong, don't give in.

SCOTT: Hi Tabitha.

TABITHA: Hi Scott.

SCOTT: Wanda…

WANDA: Scott, I don't even want to argue about it.

(Wanda looks to Tabitha who gives her a nod of encouragement.)

SCOTT: I'm not here to argue, I wanted to give you your CD's back…they were in my locker. *(He hands her several Compact Discs.)*

WANDA: Oh…well, thank you.

SCOTT: So, I guess we won't be going to the Cobra's concert this weekend.

WANDA: I think you know the answer to that.

SCOTT: Even though I already bought the tickets for us.

WANDA: *(looks to Tabitha)* Uh…No. It wouldn't be right.

SCOTT: How about you, Tabitha: You want to go?

TABITHA: Sure. *(Tabitha stands and crosses to him.)* What time you gonna pick me up?

SCOTT: Early, so we can get some dinner first.

(They start walking away.)

TABITHA: How about that new Chinese place that opened in the mall?

SCOTT: Sounds good to me.

(They are now gone, leaving a very confused Wanda sitting alone.)

SCENE 16

Annie Yeager sits nervously waiting to see the Principal, she is surprised when Denise Lowell enters and sits next to her.

ANNIE: Denise? What are you doing here?

DENISE: Mr. Kelsey kicked me out of class.

ANNIE: You were kicked out of class? Miss National Honor Society. Miss Class President. Miss everything, except Miss Behave.

DENISE: Well, today I crossed over to the other side…way over.

ANNIE: What happened?

DENISE: *Into the World Came A Soul Named Ida.*

ANNIE: Ida who?

DENISE: It's a famous painting of a homely woman…some say she's a prostitute.

ANNIE: Wow, I'm taking the wrong classes here.

DENISE: It was question #5 on our midterm final. "Explain the meaning of the painting *Into The World Came A Soul Named Ida.*"

ANNIE: And he got mad because you called Ida a prostitute?

DENISE: He got mad because I didn't. I didn't see her that way and I told him he had no right marking my answer wrong, just because I disagreed with him.

ANNIE: What did you disagree on?

DENISE: He saw Ida as a common whore, who painted herself up and struck out into the night in search of quick money.

ANNIE: How did you see her?

DENISE: I saw her as a symbol of what being a woman has always been about. The fact that we are forced to become something other than what we want to be. Ida was homely, and was looked down on by society. She was a victim of her own insecurity, but that didn't make her a whore. She was struggling in a world that imposed its values on her, just as Mr. Kelsey was imposing his views on us. And he told me I was wrong! It was my interpretation. How can I be wrong? He can expose us to paintings, but how dare he insist that we agree with what he says they mean. Suddenly something inside of me just kinda snapped. And then I told Mr. Kelsey that he could never understand what Ida represented because he was a chauvinistic pig who will still living in the 19th century with his macho head up his butt. I guess it was at that point that he sent me here.

ANNIE: You really said that to him?

DENISE: Yes, I did.

ANNIE: Whoa, and you're not even a Senior yet.

(pause)

DENISE: What did you get in trouble for?

ANNIE: I'm embarrassed to say after what you told me.

DENISE: Don't be embarrassed, we all have our causes.

ANNIE: I skipped out of 3rd period History class and went to 7-11 for a Slurpee.

(pause)

VOICE OF PRINCIPAL: *(offstage)* Miss Yeager...*Annie!*

(Annie gets up and starts to exit. She stops and turns back to Denise.)

ANNIE: But...uh...*(proud)* I did it to protest how we women have been treated throughout history. *(She gives a thumbs up to Denise, and then exits.)*

SCENE 17

Gerald works on his laptop computer; Linda enters.

LINDA: Don't even tell me you didn't do it, because I know that you did?

GERALD: *(amused)* Did what?

LINDA: You hacked the school's computer.

GERALD: There's nothing hack about me, I'm a professional.

LINDA: Yes, a professional criminal.

GERALD: No one will ever find out.

LINDA: *I* found out.

GERALD: Only because I wanted you to.

(She takes out a piece of paper; looks at it.)

LINDA: I can't believe this.

GERALD: How does it feel to get straight "A's"?

LINDA: Like I'm looking at someone else's report card, that's how it feels.

GERALD: I was going to give you a couple of "B's", but then I thought... what the heck. Let's live a little.

LINDA: They're going to find out about this.

GERALD: Never.

LINDA: Yes, they will, because I'm going right down to the office and tell them.

GERALD: I don't think you will.

LINDA: What makes you so sure?

GERALD: Scenario: Your house last night. "Linda, come in here, your Mother and I want to talk to you about your report card". Nervously you walk into the family den, head held low, sweat beads starting to form on your forehead. Knowing that the highest mark you earned was a "C", and that was in Band. Lifting your head, you become confused to see your parents smiling...beaming with pride. "We are so proud of you...we knew you could do it". The hugs, the praise, and let me guess: Money? A trip? Maybe even a shopping spree at the mall? All of this, because of a few strokes on the keyboard from yours truly. No way will you give all of that up.

LINDA: You're out of your mind.

GERALD: Very much in, thank you.

LINDA: But why? That's what I can't understand. Why did you do it?

GERALD: Because I wanted to ask you out next weekend.

LINDA: You wanted to ask me out?

GERALD: On a date, you may have low grades...but I'm sure you know what a date is.

LINDA: You broke into the computer room because you wanted to ask me out?

GERALD: I didn't break in...I have a key.

LINDA: And you thought by fixing my report card, I'd then want to go out with you?

GERALD: You now owe me.

LINDA: Owe you?

GERALD: It's a matter of logic. Like a computer game. It merely lowers the risk of failure.

LINDA: I don't believe this. It just doesn't work that way.

GERALD: It always has before.

LINDA: You've done this before?

GERALD: Four times. And those girls were all appreciative. They were glad I did it.

LINDA: Well I'm different.

GERALD: Come on, you can't tell me that you didn't get a rush when you saw all those high grades. And now that you know how talented I am, don't I look a lot better to you?

LINDA: Gerald, let me explain something to you. I don't date guys because of what they do for me. I date guys because I want to be with them.

GERALD: So, now you want to be with me, right.

LINDA: No! As a matter of fact, I want to turn you in for the slime ball that you are.

GERALD: I'll deny everything.

LINDA: I'm sure you would.

GERALD: If you tell the office, then your parents will know your real grades.

LINDA: They already do. I told them that there was a mistake on my report card. Like maybe the computer burped or something.

GERALD: Computers don't burp.

LINDA: Well, they bought it. And they were pretty disappointed with the truth. I think it made my real grades sound even worse.

GERALD: That's your own fault.

LINDA: My fault?

GERALD: You could have had good grades for the rest of the year if you want. And that's not all. How about airline tickets? A credit line at the store of your choice? Free phone calls? You name it and me and my little computer can create it.

LINDA: You are one sick puppy.

GERALD: You know, you're different than the rest. I didn't enter your attitude into the equation. I really thought I had you figured out.

LINDA: Gerald, you don't even have yourself figured out. *(She exits.)*

GERALD: So does this mean you aren't going to go out with me?

SCENE 18

Sue Powell enters.

SUE POWELL: *(smug)* I was picked as the Homecoming Queen, and you weren't. *(She exits.)*

SCENE 19

MIKE: My name is Mike. Some of you know me as Cougar, 'cause that was the name given to me by the gang. Well, it wasn't given to me, I had to earn it by doin' crimes. Like robbin' some guy over on 7th Street. He was walkin' on our sidewalk. It was like he was askin' for it. I showed him my loaded 9…and he gave up his cash. 'Cause nobody gonna disrespect me on my own turf when I got my gun. Nobody. *(pause)* And then the school here put in those damn metal detectors and I had to leave my gun at home during the day. At home where my little brother found it and decided to play with it. He must have seen me put it under the mattress when I wasn't lookin'. Jesus, he was too young to know what that thing could do—to him it was just a toy. *(pause)* I was the one that found his body. The ambulance took a long time to get to him. Ambulances always take a long time in my part of town. But it didn't matter anyway. Oh God, how did he get in my room? I locked the door. I mean I really thought I locked the door. What the hell was he doin' in there anyway? *(long pause)* Look, don't call me Cougar. I don't want that name no more. 'Cause my little brother didn't call me that. He didn't know who Cougar was. My little brother...he knew me only as Mike.

SCENE 20

CHRISTIAN: When I was a kid, my teachers told my parents that I had a bad temper. It was so much easier to deal with then. But now things have changed. Now I have a Psychiatrist who says that I suffer from "Spontaneous Emotional Episodes", which basically means...I have a bad temper. And what did this Genius, who gets paid $100 an hour, suggest I do to overcome my disorder? *Socks.* He said that I should put a sock on my hand, and have it represent the person I'm upset with. I'm supposed to tell that sock everything that bothers me about our relationship and not hold anything back. So I took his advice and focused on one person that made me angrier than all the rest. *(He puts a bright red sock on his left hand.)* I call him Dr. Shaffer, my Psychiatrist. *(To sock)* Listen you overeducated, lay-down-on-my-couch, blame-everything-on-my-Mother, $100-an-hour, out-of- shape, frustrated Freud, long-word-using, can't-get-your-own-act-together dork! I'm sick of going to your office just because I happen to get a little mad at people once and awhile and having you make me feel like I'm some sort of serial killer. *(Makes sock talk)* "But Christian, you have to learn to control your anger before you enter the real world." *(To sock)* By wearing a stupid sock on my hand and talking to it like it was a person? Is that what they do in the real world? Are you trying to heal me, or train me to be a ventriloquist? You jerk! *(Pause; takes sock off his hand)* You know something . . . maybe he's right. I do feel a lot better.

SCENE 21

Noel and Grant play catch with a football. Allison, a rather timid girl with glasses, enters and watches for a moment.

ALLISON: Grant, can I talk to you?

GRANT: You already are.

ALLISON: I mean...alone.

NOEL: Whoa...

(He laughs suggestively, causing Allison to shoot him a dirty look.)

GRANT: *(to Noel)* I'll catch up with you later, Noel.

NOEL: Alright, but if I run into Jacqueline, I may just have to tell her about you two.

GRANT: Get lost.

(Noel leaves, but not before giving Allison another heckling laugh.)

GRANT: You got two minutes.

ALLISON: I should have said something in front of him...I should have said something in front of the whole class.

GRANT: What are you talkin' about?

ALLISON: I saw you Grant Arthur...I saw you cheating on the test this morning.

GRANT: That's bull, I didn't cheat on no test.

ALLISON: I sit right behind you, I saw you copy from Kenneth. You weren't even subtle about it. He would write his answer, and then you'd copy, he'd write, you'd copy...you even turned your test in right after he did.

GRANT: I don't have to take this from you. *(He starts to leave.)*

ALLISON: If I don't get some answers, I'll go to Mr. Martin and tell him. All he has to do is compare your tests and he'd know.

(Grant stops.)

GRANT: So...you saw me copying off someone's test. What do you care? I didn't copy off from you.

ALLISON: Oh, then it shouldn't matter because I wasn't involved?

GRANT: Yeah, what's it to you?

ALLISON: Because I studied last night, that's why.

GRANT: What?

ALLISON: I know you won't believe this, but I have a life, too. There was a movie I wanted to go to last night, but I couldn't because I had to stay home and study "mitosis".

GRANT: Mitosis?

ALLISON: Mitosis…It was the 7th question on the test, you wrote down "C", which was the correct answer.

GRANT: How do you know I wrote down "C"? Were you copying off my paper?

ALLISON: Don't twist this around…I studied.

GRANT: I remember about Mitosis. Mr. Martin showed that movie. The nucleus of a cell divides in half and each of the halves contain the same number of chromosomes.

ALLISON: *(surprised)* That's right.

GRANT: I know.

ALLISON: If you knew that, then why did you have to copy Kenneth's test?

GRANT: Maybe I just did it for grins.

ALLISON: Grins?

GRANT: Yeah, as a joke.

ALLISON: I don't buy that for a minute. Why did you cheat?

GRANT: *(impatient)* The same reason I cheat on every test I take.

ALLISON: Don't tell me, you're worried about getting kicked off the football team. You jocks are all alike.

GRANT: You're way out of line.

ALLISON: *(angry)* If that isn't the reason, then what is?

GRANT: *(returning anger)* If you really have to know, it's because I can't read.

ALLISON: What?

(Grant looks around to make sure no one heard him.)

GRANT: Look if you want to turn me in, go ahead. Just leave me alone. *(He starts to exit.)*

ALLISON: Wait.

(He stops; Allison crosses to him.)

ALLISON: I'm not going to turn you in. It just made me a little angry when I saw you get away with it, that's all.

GRANT: Yeah, well I've been getting away with it for a long time.

ALLISON: You really can't read?

GRANT: I can read…a little. Easy stuff. But it takes me awhile and tests use a lot of big words…Listen, I shouldn't have said anything. You tricked me.

ALLISON: If you're worried about me telling anyone, forget it. I'm not like that. I just can't imagine that someone who's gone to school as long as you wouldn't be able to read.

GRANT: It's easier than you think.

ALLISON: They have special programs that could help.

GRANT: And what do they call kids that go to these special programs?

ALLISON: *(sarcastic)* Wouldn't want people to make fun of you, I mean being so popular and all.

GRANT: So, are you pissed because I cheated on the test, or because I'm popular?

ALLISON: I'm sorry, I didn't mean it that way.

GRANT: Look if it makes you feel better. Next test Martin gives, I'll flunk it.

ALLISON: That won't make me feel better.

GRANT: Then what do you want from me?

(pause)

ALLISON: Let me help you.

GRANT: Help me?

ALLISON: I could help you to read...better, I mean.

GRANT: No way.

ALLISON: No one would need to know, you could come over to my place. We've got a guest house out back that no one ever uses. We could work there.

GRANT: It's too late, maybe a few years ago.

ALLISON: Grant, you're a very smart guy, I can tell. It wouldn't take long...I know it wouldn't.

GRANT: But what if someone finds out?

ALLISON: You've gone all this time and no one did.

GRANT: I'll have to think about this.

ALLISON: Alright, I won't push it. But you'd also be doing me a favor.

GRANT: How?

ALLISON: I plan on teaching someday, it would be good practice.

GRANT: Yeah, well...like I said, I'll think about it.

ALLISON: Okay. *(She starts to head off.)*

GRANT: Allison?

ALLISON: Yes?

GRANT: We got a game tonight, but...how about tomorrow around eight?

ALLISON: That would be fine.

GRANT: Great...thanks. *(Grant looks around, then exits.)*

Pamela and Jennifer enter.

JENNIFER: Do you mind if I sit down?

PAMELA: Maybe you need some food.

JENNIFER: The cafeteria is too crowded.

PAMELA: So we make room, I think you should eat.

JENNIFER: Just give me a minute here. I mean I've only been out of the hospital a few days.

PAMELA: Yeah, but you're fine now.

JENNIFER: Do you think I look pale?

PAMELA: Not anymore than usual. I swear you're part albino.

JENNIFER: I don't know. Kim told me I looked pale.

PAMELA: She spends her life out in the sun, everybody looks pale to her. Let's go eat.

(Pamela starts to leave, Jennifer doesn't move.)

JENNIFER: You didn't say anything to anybody, did you?

PAMELA: I told you I wouldn't.

JENNIFER: People have been treating me different.

PAMELA: You've had two weeks off from school, they're just jealous.

JENNIFER: I feel so different. Just like that I'm some kind of freak.

PAMELA: Come on, you have Diabetes. Lot's of people have it. My Aunt has it.

JENNIFER: You're Aunt doesn't go to this High School.

PAMELA: I think the best thing for you is to eat lunch with me and catch up on all the gossip.

JENNIFER: I don't really want to be around a lot of people right now.

PAMELA: What about all your friends? *(pointed)* What about Todd? You can't avoid him for very long. This school isn't that big.

JENNIFER: I'm not avoiding Todd.

PAMELA: He thinks you are.

JENNIFER: You talked to him?

PAMELA: Third period.

JENNIFER: You didn't say anything about…if you said anything…

PAMELA: Easy, easy. I promised you I wouldn't and my word is good. I don't have much else, that at least is still worth something.

JENNIFER: What did he say?

PAMELA: He thinks you don't like him anymore.

JENNIFER: Oh, God. He's so insecure sometimes.

PAMELA: Insecure? You miss two weeks of school, don't return his calls, and then when you come back to school you're like the Invisible Woman or something.

JENNIFER: I'm just not ready to tell him yet.

PAMELA: What's to tell? So you have to take a few shots. *(dramatic)* With great big needles!

(Jennifer shoots her a look.)

PAMELA: Just kidding. Geez, I'm just trying to lighten things up here.

JENNIFER: You make it sound like I caught a cold or something. I'm a little scared, okay. Two weeks ago everything was fine, then I get the flu and all of a sudden I'm being rushed to the hospital and they tell me I have some kind of disease that I know nothing about. I thought it was because I ate too much candy, but they say it has something to do with genetics and blood lines and stuff I don't want to think of. The next thing I know I'm sticking a syringe into an orange and watching tapes of blind people with their legs cut off. Excuse me if I think it is a big deal.

PAMELA: Todd really cares about you, Jennifer. He's hurting right now.

JENNIFER: And you think if I tell him I have a major disease, that will make everything alright?

PAMELA: Something like that.

JENNIFER: And the two of us will just go on being boyfriend and girlfriend like nothing has happened.

PAMELA: Why not?

JENNIFER: Your Aunt's diabetic...so is my cousin. Thought everything was going to be fine, until one night during a Valentine's Dance she passed out on the dance floor and they had to call the paramedics. Her boyfriend was real understanding...he understood it was too embarrassing to be with her in public. Dropped her within a week.

PAMELA: So your cousin went with a jerk, you're going with Todd.

JENNIFER: Why did this have to happen to me?

PAMELA: Look at the bright side, at least you got a great excuse to get out of gym class when Miss Ulmer gets her panties in a wad.

(Jennifer stifles a laugh on that.)

PAMELA: He's going to find out...it might as well be from you.

JENNIFER: Do you know where he is...

PAMELA: Cafeteria, third table, second seat...but I didn't tell him why you were going to meet him.

JENNIFER: You set me up.

PAMELA: Guilty.

JENNIFER: Oh, you are so sneaky.

PAMELA: Come on, I'll even give up my dessert in honor of you.

JENNIFER: Wow, now that really touches my heart. *(Jennifer puts her arm around Pamela, leads her off.)*

PAMELA: But just for lunch. Tonight I plan on pigging out on cookies, a hot fudge sundae, frozen yogurt topped with Gummi Bears, crushed oreos…

(They are now gone.)

SCENE 23
Allen paces, Marisa sits.

ALLEN: What's taking them so long? We should have known an hour ago.

MARISA: Maybe it's closer than you think.

ALLEN: Maybe it's such a landslide that they have to think of a nice way to break the news to you.

MARISA: You're pretty confident.

ALLEN: I'm the best man for the job.

MARISA: Best *man?*

ALLEN: You know what I mean…but leave it to you to try to twist everything I say, just like you did throughout the whole campaign.

MARISA: I may have twisted, but I never lied like you did.

ALLEN: Name one thing I lied about.

MARISA: Matching funds for field trips…longer lunch periods…your scholastic record…

ALLEN: I said name one thing.

MARISA: So you admit to those lies?

ALLEN: They weren't lies, they were campaign promises…if the President of the United States can stretch the truth, why not the President of the Senior Class?

MARISA: They haven't elected you yet.

ALLEN: They will. *(pause)* Listen, I know the campaign got a little rough…

MARISA: A little rough? You spray painted graffiti on my car, you appointed my ex-boyfriend as your campaign advisor so you could dig up dirt on me, and you spread rumors that I was having an affair with the School Superintendent.

ALLEN: You do spend a lot of time in his office.

MARISA: My Mother is his Secretary.

ALLEN: Hey, that's politics.

MARISA: You're nothing but a *Slimeball.* You ran a very dirty campaign.

ALLEN: You're starting to sound like a sore loser. Does that mean you're conceding?

MARISA: Never.

ALLEN: You have to admit, I'm exactly what the Senior Class needs.

MARISA: A loud mouth, self-important jerk?

ALLEN: Name me one politician who isn't.

MARISA: What our class needs is someone who can make some positive changes.

ALLEN: Campaign's over. Save it for your next failed attempt at Government.

MARISA: Failed attempt? What about you? As I remember, you ran for President, and lost, for the past three years.

ALLEN: Not true. My Sophomore year I ran for Treasurer.

MARISA: That's right, Treasurer. Now I remember…and I voted for you.

ALLEN: You did?

MARISA: I thought you were the best *person* for the job.

ALLEN: Really?

MARISA: Really.

ALLEN: Why did you think that?

MARISA: We were both in Geometry class. It was a Tuesday—I remember the day because Mr. Talma was giving his weekly pop quiz—you sat a few seats in front of me and right behind Linda Jansen. She had slung her purse across the back of her chair and a twenty dollar bill fell out. You picked it up and stuffed it back in her purse. Didn't even tell her about it, just put it back in her purse.

ALLEN: See, I'm a wonderful guy.

MARISA: You were back then, but you've changed.

ALLEN: Just because I play the politician doesn't mean I'm like that for real.

MARISA: I don't think you can separate the two?

ALLEN: What about you? You pretend to be so honest, and so pure. What's in this for you?

MARISA: What do you mean?

ALLEN: Nobody runs for office, even in High School, without wanting something in return. Is it power? Is it greed? Or is it knowing that everyone will kiss your butt for favors?

MARISA: You have an evil mind.

ALLEN: Maybe, but at least I'm willing to admit my lust for power.

MARISA: I want to be Class President to help my fellow students.

ALLEN: I don't believe you. And that's what bothers you the most about me. *(A student enters.)*

STUDENT: Congratulations Marisa, you're the new Class President. *(Long pause; Marisa is as stunned as Allen.)*

ALLEN: How close was it?

STUDENT: Well, we're not really supposed to tell.

ALLEN: *(angry)* I demand a recount. *(To student)* Especially if you had anything to do with counting the votes.

STUDENT: Oh yeah, well if you really have to know, she creamed you. You only got about 10% of the votes. *(Student leaves.)*

MARISA: Allen, I'm sorry.

ALLEN: No you're not. *(pause)* Aw, what the hell...the people have spoken. *(He starts to leave.)*

MARISA: Wait. You were right. I did want this position for a reason. I thought it would look good on my record...that a college might give me special consideration because of it.

ALLEN: Well, maybe there's hope for you yet.

MARISA: You know I really didn't think I'd win.

ALLEN: Neither did I.

MARISA: It's a big responsibility. I'm a little naive about all of this. I could use your help.

ALLEN: My help? You called me a slimeball.

MARISA: You are...I mean part of you is. And that's why I need your help.

ALLEN: What's in it for me?

MARISA: As much power as I can throw your way.

ALLEN: You've only been in office for a few minutes, and you've already made your first good decision.

SCENE 24

Adam spots Vera, runs to her and gives her a big kiss.

VERA: I've missed you.

ADAM: How long has it been?

VERA: Almost ten hours.

ADAM: That's too long.

VERA: Way too long.

(Adam notices her small diamond ring.)

ADAM: I thought you weren't going to wear that.

VERA: Not at home, but I'm going to here at school.

ADAM: Aren't you afraid that someone will find out?

VERA: To tell the truth, I'm afraid someone won't.

ADAM: I still think we should tell our parents.

VERA: You know I do too, but we both agreed that your Dad would freak.

ADAM: No, my Mom would freak, my Dad would probably disown me.

VERA: They're gonna really hate me when they find out.

ADAM: Then it's their problem, not yours.

VERA: Well, for now they'll just have to settle on not liking me. Even though I am their daughter-in-law.

(Adam takes a couple of steps away.)

VERA: What's wrong?

ADAM: It's not fair to ask you to be my wife and then pretend that we're still just dating.

VERA: We've been all through this. It's only for a couple more months, then we're both 18 and nobody can say nothing.

ADAM: You're right.

VERA: No, *we're* right.

ADAM: So do you feel any different?

VERA: I didn't think I would, but when I woke up today…I can't even describe it.

ADAM: You don't have to…been there, done that.

VERA: You don't regret it, do you?

ADAM: No way, it's perfect. We're perfect.

VERA: I still want a big wedding, you know.

ADAM: I know. You want the beauty of an old-fashioned wedding.

VERA: No, I want the appliances and money and stuff.

ADAM: *(smiling)* Now I see.

VERA: Besides, keeping this thing a secret, you know, living each day like a mystery…it's so romantic.

ADAM: I never looked at it like that before. It is kinda like a movie or something.

VERA: One with a very happy ending.

(They look at each other for a moment. Then they embrace and kiss.)

VERA: It will always be like this, won't it Adam.

ADAM: Always.

(He puts his arm around her and they exit.)

SCENE 25

Deidra and Brent sit next to each other; each wears a Graduation Cap and robe.

VOICE: *(offstage)* As you travel down the road of life, you will find that the years spent here at this school will become a foundation for your success. In the future, when you look back, you will remember these to be the best of times and the worst of times… *(Voice fades.)*

DEIDRA: *(Whispers)* I can't believe we made it. Finally after twelve years of sitting in classes, we are free. First thing I'm gonna do is sleep until noon tomorrow. *(pause)* God this speaker is boring, why did they get him?

BRENT: He's a politician.

DEIDRA: Personally I think they should have gotten a VJ from MTV… that's someone I'd listen to.

BRENT: It's not for us, it's for our parents.

DEIDRA: My Mom watches MTV.

BRENT: Your Mom's not a typical parent.

DEIDRA: Besides, I thought he was supposed to speak before we got our diplomas.

BRENT: He was late getting here…they flew him in on a helicopter.

DEIDRA: When you're a kid and you're late it's called being tardy…when you get older it's called being important.

BRENT: Yeah, right.

DEIDRA: You having a party tonight?

BRENT: No.

DEIDRA: Saving it for the weekend so all the relatives will come?

BRENT: Well...uh...not exactly.

DEIDRA: I'm having mine tonight, you can come over if you want. I can't wait to score all that cash.

BRENT: At least you're honest.

DEIDRA: So are your parents going to get you that car like they promised?

BRENT: Not for awhile.

DEIDRA: You oughta sue 'em. They promised you a car when you graduated. They can't back out of a deal like that.

BRENT: They haven't backed out. I didn't graduate yet.

DEIDRA: What are you talking about? We just picked up our diplomas. Of course you graduated.

BRENT: Mine's not signed.

DEIDRA: What do you mean it's not signed?

(He shows her.)

DEIDRA: It's not signed.

BRENT: Just like I said.

(Deidra looks at her own diploma.)

DEIDRA: Mine is...they must have made some mistake on yours.

BRENT: It was no mistake. I'm a credit short. I have to go to summer school.

DEIDRA: How can you be a credit short?

BRENT: I flunked Spanish class.

DEIDRA: I thought you said you were passing all of your classes.

BRENT: I thought I was too.

DEIDRA: When did you find out?

BRENT: Two days ago. My parents got a letter in the mail.

DEIDRA: A letter?

BRENT: I wasn't too happy about that either. Here I am, eighteen years old...old enough to vote, but I guess not old enough to handle this kind of news.

DEIDRA: They're probably afraid you wouldn't tell your parents about it.

BRENT: One things for sure, I sure wouldn't have until after I got the car.

DEIDRA: That bites, just because you flunked Spanish. I could see if it was English you flunked, but Spanish? What's that matter?

BRENT: I guess now since most of our jobs are going to Mexico, it's really important.

DEIDRA: You got a point there.

BRENT: I really didn't want to be here today, but the school sorta made me.

DEIDRA: They made you come to the ceremony, even though you're not done yet? That's cruel.

BRENT: They told my parents I should be here since they don't have a graduation ceremony in August. Besides my mom already bought a new dress for today…that's what she was the most pissed about.

DEIDRA: Well, she got to wear it then. What about your dad?

BRENT: He's pretty disappointed in me. He didn't say much, but I can tell because he didn't bring his video camera. He takes that every-where. I heard him tell my Mom he didn't want any footage of me receiving an unsigned diploma.

DEIDRA: No one would have to know, it's not like that would show on the video.

BRENT: I'm glad he's not recording this. I don't need to be reminded ten years from now what a loser I was.

DEIDRA: You're not a loser.

BRENT: Easy for you to say, your diploma is signed.

(They both stand up. They are joined by all of the other cast members, who also wear graduation caps and gowns. They all form a line across the stage, facing the audience; Deidra and Brent are in the center.)

DEIDRA: Hey, look…I'm pretty good at Spanish. If you want, I could tutor you this summer.

BRENT: I may need that.

DEIDRA: As long as it's not before noon.

BRENT: Don't rub it in.

VOICE: *(offstage)* The world is our oyster and it's up to each and every one of you to open it up and grab hold of the pearl that you've worked so hard for. My respect and encouragement goes out to you the class of_____!

(All the cast members remove their graduation caps and throw them into the air, as the lights fade to black.)

END OF PLAY

THE LESS THAN HUMAN CLUB
by Timothy Mason

BIOGRAPHY

Timothy Mason lives and works in New York City. His plays include *The Fiery Furnace,* which premiered in New York at the Lucille Lortel Theatre, with Julie Harris; *Babylon Gardens,* with Timothy Hutton and Mary-Louise Parker at Circle Rep; *Ascension Day,* commissioned and produced by ACT's Young Conservatory in San Francisco; *Only You,* Circle Rep; *Bearclaw,* Seattle Rep's Second Stage; *Levitation,* Circle Rep; and *In a Northern Landscape,* which was first produced by the Actors Theatre of Louisville. He has also written many stage adaptations of young peoples' classics for the Minneapolis Children's Theater Company, including *How the Grinch Stole Christmas, The 500 Hats of Bartholomew Cubbins, Treasure Island, The Adventures of Tom Sawyer,* and a dozen others.

Timothy has won a W. Alton Jones Foundation grant, the Kennedy Center's Fund for New American Plays Award, a playwriting fellowship from the National Endowment for the Arts, a Hollywood Drama-Logue Award, the Twin Cities Drama Critics Award, and a National Society of Arts and Letters Award.

AUTHOR'S NOTE

I recently taught a playwrights' workshop at a large state university. One day, before meeting with a group of young writers, I stood on the campus watching a hummingbird at close range. As it gathered sustenance from some citrus blossoms, its movements were a brilliant iridescent blur; so rapid, so frantic, such a struggle. Later one of the students asked if it was hard to make a living as a playwright. I said that yes, it is hard to be a playwright, but it's harder to be a hummingbird.

If I had been asked if it is difficult to be a human being, I would say yes, but it's harder to be a young human being.

When Craig Slaight called me early in 1994 to commission a play for ACT's Young Conservatory, I told him I didn't have a clue what I might write, but I wanted very much to do it. I had had a remarkable time four years earlier, writing *Ascension Day* for him, and working with his young actors as they put that story on its feet and gave it life.

I went to bed that night with the sort of fear a writer feels when he or she hasn't a single idea, and woke up the next morning with a chant: "Nathan Hale High—Not Hardly Human." I had dreamt a play, one of those occasional experiences that make my life easier than a humming-bird's.

A decade earlier I had written an autobiographical play, *Levitation*, and afterward felt great relief that I wouldn't have to do *that* again. I had told my own story, or a piece of it, and could turn my attention to other peoples' stories. But as I worked on *The Less Than Human Club*, I realized that it was happening again: Here and there scenes felt painfully familiar, and characters were all but saying, "It's good to see you again, Tim. How've you been?" I was reliving, to an extent, a few moment of my youth.

That it is difficult to be a young human today is terribly evident. It was also difficult to be young in the turbulence of the late 1960s. What was remarkable to me, in the course of rehearsals in San Francisco, mid-1990s, was discovering how closely the young actors were able to relate to the pains, frustrations, defeats, and joys of their 60s counterparts. Again and again the kids would say, "It's just the same, I know these people, I am one of these people."

It should not have been surprising, of course. Even though a teacher today could hardly get away with beating his students, as we were beaten—regularly, viciously—by a junior high gym instructor, young people today are still being given the message, insidiously, that they are somehow less than human. By virtue of their age, their lack of status, their powerlessness.

This message, to cite just one example, is sent by a society that pays great lip service to its children while showing ever less inclination to pay for their education. If the children in question are poor, nonwhite, and/or foreign, they can damn well starve. This is a powerful message. And if children today are taught that they don't count for much, they are also learning by inference that human life counts for little, and that it's acceptable to treat as less than human persons of another race, another gender, another sexual orientation.

The young actors who brought this play to life, who study and work and perform at Craig Slaight's Young Conservatory, are being taught quite a different lesson. There, at ACT, they count for very much, indeed. They are fully human, and treated as such. And through their work on stage, they are enabled to exalt the worth of the human animal in all its struggling, iridescent variations.

Timothy Mason
October 12, 1995

ORIGINAL PRODUCTION

The Less Than Human Club was commissioned and first presented by the Young Conservatory at the american Conservatory Theater (Carey Perloff, Artistic Director), San Francisco, California, in August 1994. It was directed by Craig Slaight; costumes designed by Callie Floor; lighting designed by Kelly Roberson; the assistant director was Paul Shikany. The cast was as follows:

Davis Daniels	Kevin Crook
Clinton Armstrong	Domenic Manchester
Harley DeYoung	Niels Kirk
Amanda Denney	Kristin Schwartz
Dan Dwyer	Michael Smith
Julie Nyquist	Lauren Hodges
Kirsten Sabo	Maria Sideris
Melissa Armstrong	Felicia Benefield

CHARACTERS

Davis Daniels
Clinton Armstrong
Harley DeYoung
Amanda Denney
Dan Dwyer
Julie Nyquist
Kirsten Sabo
Melissa Armstrong

All are high school juniors, about 17-years-old, except for Clinton's sister Melissa, 14, a freshman.

TIME

Fall of 1967; winter and spring of 1968.

THE LESS THAN
HUMAN CLUB

1. HOMECOMING

DAVIS: *(to us)* It was right out of the blue. I got a postcard. Or rather, my mother did, I don't live here anymore. She read it to me over the phone. There are some words that are a crossing of the border, one human being to another. Whole can of slippery worms. And suddenly there's such a lot of unfinished business. I'm getting ahead of myself. Autumn, 1967. I'll get to the postcard, if I can.

CLINTON: *(over public address system)* "Freshmen." *(Clinton raps on the microphone, and if that doesn't make "feedback" noises, Clinton makes them himself.)* "Freshmen. Principal Withers here. Nathan Hale High welcomes you."

DAVIS: *(to us)* Nathan Hale was a spy.

CLINTON: *(over PA)* "Walk tall. Keep your noses clean. The longest journey begins with a single step. Look lively. Get the lead out."

DAVIS: Our school is named after a spy.

CLINTON: *(over PA)* "Sophomores. You know the rules by now. You know the ropes. I expect you to tow the line, I expect you to pull your weight. So get your ducks in a row and keep 'em there."

DAVIS: When we don't have anything better to do, we all go to Nathan Hale High. Principal Withers likes to call it "NHH."

CLINTON: *(over PA)* "Juniors."

AMANDA: Look out, here it comes.

CLINTON: "Pitfalls ahead. Beware Junior Slump."

DAN: *(doing a sort of Richard III routine)* Oh, my god, I think I've—someone, help me—I've got Junior Slump!

CLINTON: "We the staff, faculty and custodial technicians here at NHH have seen juniors come, and we've seen 'em fall on their faces. Complacent. Smug. Know-it-all. Just remember this, NHH juniors: the Russians are watching."

DAVIS: Principal Withers is big on the Russians. The guy on the mike is Clinton. Clinton is big on Principal Withers.

CLINTON: *(to us)* Hi.

DAVIS: We call Clinton "Scarecrow."

CLINTON: Do not. Do that.

DAVIS: Clinton calls Principal Withers "Old Waddle-Butt."

CLINTON: *(over PA)* "Seniors. Glory awaits you. A shimmering sunrise of hope and achievement and wholesome young American manhood and womanhood. It's up to you. You can have it, sSeniors. Or you can choose shame, degradation and early hair loss."

AMANDA: Can I have the degradation without the hair loss?

DAN: Jake? We'll have the degradation special, hold the hair loss.

CLINTON: *(over PA)* "Altogether now: *Nathan Hale! NHH! Nathan Hale! NHH!* I can't hear you! *Nathan Hale! NHH!*"
(Julie and Kirsten execute elaborate cheerleader maneuvers with pom-poms.)

JULIE & KIRSTEN & CLINTON: *Nathan Hale! NHH! Nathan Hale! NHH! Nathan Hale! NHH!*

HARLEY: Oh, blow it out your ass.
(Sudden shocked silence.)

CLINTON: *(over PA)* "I heard that. You think I didn't hear that?"

DAVIS: *(to us)* Harley DeYoung was the only member of our group to have his own probation officer. He was the baddest white boy in our class. I was in love with him. I wanted to tell him. Words may be cheap, but they weren't back then.

CLINTON: What is this "white boy" stuff, Davis. You got a separate category for Negroes?

DAVIS: Sometimes, Clinton. So do you. *(To us)* Clinton was the whitest Negro in our class.

CLINTON: That's not funny.

DAVIS: Clinton was the one person I could really talk to and I never did.

CLINTON: That's not funny, it's not true.

DAVIS: I think of all the things I should have said to him and didn't.

CLINTON: I mean it, Davis.

DAVIS: Clinton, shut up. Anyway, you can't hear me, you've been dead for years.

CLINTON: *(after a beat)* That's really not funny.

DAVIS: I'm telling you, you didn't hear it.

CLINTON: *(over the PA, impersonating Principal Withers again)* "You think I didn't hear that, Harley, I heard that."

DAVIS: Pssst. Harley. NHH—Not Hardly Human.

HARLEY: *NHH, Not Hardly Human, NHH, Not Hardly Human!*

JULIE: Oh god.

KIRSTEN: Harley, shut up.

HARLEY & AMANDA: *NHH, Not Hardly Human...*

HARLEY & AMANDA & DAN: *NHH, Not Hardly Human, NHH, Not Hardly Human...*

CLINTON: *(over PA)* "Fine. Off to a fine start".

KIRSTEN: Very funny, Harley.

DAVIS: That's how it started, our club.

AMANDA: Don't call it a club, god why is he calling it a club?

DAVIS: I know how you turned out, too, Mandy.

AMANDA: My name is Amanda, okay?

DAVIS: You're nothing like what you thought you'd be.

AMANDA: Don't say that. Why would you say that? I have dreams, dammit. Don't say that.

DAVIS: *(to Amanda)* I'm sorry. For everything.

CLINTON: *(over PA)* "Harley DeYoung?"

AMANDA: Why is he saying that? "Club" sounds so pathetic, like kids in a treehouse or something.

DAVIS: For a while we called it the Not Hardly Human Club, between classes we'd get together in Jake's Place across the street and fry our minds on caffeine and nicotine and onion rings, and that's what we called it for a couple of weeks that fall.

AMANDA: Hey Jake, who do you have to screw to get a refill?

KIRSTEN: How can you *talk* like that? How can she talk like that?

DAVIS: Oh just—You know, Kirsten? Maybe someday you'll be able to say whatever you want to say, maybe someday you won't be so damned uptight.

KIRSTEN: I suppose that's some kind of hippy word. My dad says hippies are fems.

DAVIS: Here's good news, though, Kirsten: I have no idea what happened to you. I barely remember you.

KIRSTEN: That's not very nice. I remember you.

DAVIS: Do you really? Or is that just my ego talking.

KIRSTEN: I remember.

DAVIS: *(to us)* Fall of '67. I can't remember who changed it to The Less Than Human Club.

HARLEY: You did. You said it sounded better.

DAVIS: Oh, yeah. Hey, Harley. Thanks for the postcard, it meant the earth to me.

HARLEY: What postcard?

DAVIS: Oh, yeah, right. I'll get to the postcard, I'll try. *(To us)* Earlier that summer race riots had erupted all over the country. Cities burned, nearly a hundred were killed, mostly black. Even here they called out the National Guard. But that fall we were locked into a fortress named for the man who regretted he had but one life to give for his country, and we hardly heard a whisper.

CLINTON: *(over PA)* "Harley DeYoung, I'll see you in my office at ten-hundred hours. Sharp."

DAVIS: Anyway, Nathan Hale was a spy. Of course he was on our side, he was working for the good guys, but still.

HARLEY: Wait a minute, wait a minute. You think it's fun?

DAN: What's fun?

HARLEY: It wasn't even my idea, but who catches holy hell for it as usual?

DAN: Nothing's ever your idea, Harley.

HARLEY: You all think it's so damn funny, Oh god, Harley's going to the Principal's office again.

DAVIS: Harley? Excuse me. I'm trying to explain something here.

HARLEY: He makes me feel small. He's worse than Coach Knipsy.

DAN: Nobody's worse than Coach Knipsy.

AMANDA: Old Popeye arms.

DAN: Mr. Whip.

JULIE: He really does that? He really hits you?

CLINTON: The Lanyard Lasher.

DAN: The Ping-Pong Paddler.
    (Harley exits.)

JULIE: Now that's something I'd like to see.

CLINTON: I'll bet you would.

JULIE: Could you get me into the boys' locker room sometime?

DAN: Julie, since when have you needed help getting into the boys' locker room?

AMANDA: What is he, a pervert or something?

DAN: Nah. He just hates kids.

DAVIS: You're so in love with Mandy it hurts, right, Dan?

DAN: Shut up, Davis.

AMANDA: Shut up, Davis. And it's *Amanda*. Is this going be all about who's secretly in love with who? Cause that's about as boring as it gets.

DAVIS: Things like that can be important.

AMANDA: I really expected more from you, Davis.

DAVIS: Hey! Do you want to do this or not?

DAN: Well…

AMANDA: Frankly…

CLINTON: I've got a chemistry exam in the morning…

DAVIS: Okay, okay, bad question. *I* want to do this, okay?

AMANDA: Well…

DAN: Frankly…

CLINTON: I've got a chemistry exam in the morning…

DAVIS: Geez, you people, you're…

EVERYONE ELSE: *(not unison)* Less than human!

(Everyone but Davis leaves.)

DAVIS: You're like kids in a treehouse! Kids! Secret passwords! Disappearing ink!

(Davis is alone.)

DAVIS: You're like kids in a treehouse, and it's our club and we all belong and no one else can get in and ruin it and you're more important to me than anybody ever will be in my whole life and in a couple of years I'll hardly remember your names. Disappearing ink. *(To us)* He was a schoolteacher. Nathan Hale. I forget where he came from. He was just a guy, maybe when he was a kid he liked school so much he decided he'd stay in school forever. I guess maybe he could've, if life didn't always bust in the door and ruin everything. When the revolution came, he stopped teaching school and started fighting. He became a captain in George Washington's revolutionary army. He was only twenty-one. That's when he volunteered to spy on the British.

(Amanda and Kirsten cross, carrying schoolbooks.)

KIRSTEN: He is so cute.

AMANDA: Really.

DAVIS: They dressed him up as a young Dutchman and sent him off to New York.

AMANDA: I would love to go to New York and never come back.

DAVIS: *(to us)* That's pretty much what Nathan Hale did.

AMANDA: We're going to Jake's. See you there?

DAVIS: Is the Pope infallible?

KIRSTEN: Cute but weird.

(The girls drop their books on a table at Jake's Place and sit.)

DAVIS: So they dressed him up as a young Dutch schoolmaster and he traveled down the Hudson River to New York, into enemy territory, and he drew maps and estimated troop strength and a relative of his, a cousin or something, spotted him and ratted on him to the British and the next day they put a rope around his neck and hanged him. It's my school, right, so I'm always trying to figure out, what's the moral of this story, what do we learn here? Don't ever go to New York? Avoid Dutch-boy drag? Stay away from family, they'll screw you every time? I don't know. *(Davis starts to leave.)* Don't ever spy on anyone, not even if God is on your side. *(Davis leaves.)*

2.

A day in September. Jake's Place. Amanda and Kirsten sit together at a table. We hear a distant solo jazz trumpet. Clinton brings cups of coffee for Amanda and Kirsten and sits. In the course of the following, Dan brings a tray with food and two cups of coffee, sets the tray in front of Clinton and then stands, sipping his coffee and picking onion rings off the tray.

AMANDA: I'm ready to kill Miss Borders, I really am.

KIRSTEN: Miss Borders—her earrings alone!

CLINTON: *(to Dan)* An order of rings says Harley gets detention for a week.

DAN: Two weeks. I'll see your onion rings and raise you a Coke.

AMANDA: *(to Kirsten)* I'm not talking about earrings.

CLINTON: I'll see your Coke and raise you a cole slaw.

AMANDA: I'm talking about two hours of homework three nights a week.

DAN: I don't like cole slaw.

AMANDA: Just cause *she* doesn't have a social life...

CLINTON: Cole slaw's good for you.

DAN: So's electroshock therapy.

KIRSTEN: They've gotta be straight from Woolworths.

AMANDA: Woolworth's basement, honey. It's her one-stop fashion outlet.

CLINTON: *(meaning the jazz trumpeter)* Listen.

KIRSTEN: He's been at it since the first week. Anybody know who he is?

AMANDA: You just assume it's a guy, right?

DAN: He's really good.

AMANDA: Yes, she is. You planning on joining us, Danny?

CLINTON: He can't sit down.

DAN: Shut up, Scarecrow.

CLINTON: He told Coach Knipsy his arms look like Popeye's.

KIRSTEN: To his face? How could you do that?

DAN: I just feel like standing, okay?

CLINTON: A cheeseburger deluxe says you won't be able to sit for three days.

DAN: You're on.

KIRSTEN: I don't get it.

AMANDA: God, Kirsten, you're just destined to get the Nobel Prize for swift.

KIRSTEN: What?

AMANDA: *(to Dan)* You okay?

DAN: I'm fine.

CLINTON: Knipsy made him touch his toes in the shower.

DAN: Great, Clint, if there's ever anything I can do for *you*...

KIRSTEN: Oh, my god, he *hit* you? Naked?

CLINTON: No, Coach was fully dressed. "Touch the toes, smart-ass."

AMANDA: What'd he use?

DAN: Oh, come on...

CLINTON: Lanyard. In the gym, he uses the paddle; in the showers...

AMANDA: Cheeseburgers for a week if you show us.

DAN: You are clearly a sick woman.

KIRSTEN: My uncle got hemorrhoids? And he carried around this rubber doughnut so he could sit down.

DAN: Shut up! Just...! Okay, nobody has to know about this, okay? Please? I'm asking you.

CLINTON: Sure.

AMANDA: Okay. I think it's great what you did.

DAN: Oh right.

CLINTON: It *was,* it was amazing. "Coach, I'm doing this survey for Civics class? And I need to know, what cartoon character do you feel closest to?"

AMANDA: No! That's great!

KIRSTEN: So who did he choose?

(They all look at Kirsten.)

KIRSTEN: Oh! Popeye! Of course! I guess I feel closest to Bambi.

AMANDA: There she'll be, Kirsten, winging her way to Stockholm, working on her acceptance speech...

DAN: So—code of silence?

AMANDA: Nobody but us will ever know.

(Davis enters with a cup of coffee.)

AMANDA: Hi.

DAVIS: What's up, Dan—sore butt?

DAN: Screw you.

DAVIS: *(meaning the trumpeter)* Anybody know who that is?

DAN: It's coming from the Music Annex.

CLINTON: Duh.

DAVIS: What's that he's playing?

KIRSTEN: Trumpet—oh.

CLINTON: *(to Kirsten)* Double-duh. *(to Davis) Tangerine?*

AMANDA: And it's not a he, it's a she, and she's beautiful and cool and she's got long sandy-colored hair and I want her for my best friend.

DAN: Tangerine?

(Julie enters.)

CLINTON: Not the fruit, Danny, the tune. Davis is the fruit.

DAVIS: *(after a beat)* That's not funny.

AMANDA: It really isn't, Clint.

JULIE: Hi-hi.

CLINTON: And I hate to tell you, Mandy...

AMANDA: *(overlapping)* My name is Amanda.

CLINTON: *(overlapping)*...but your new best girlfriend up there with the sandy-blond hair is a Negro male.

DAVIS: You've seen him?

CLINTON: I don't have to see him: this is not a white woman playing that horn.

AMANDA: God, that is so prejudiced.

KIRSTEN: *(to Julie)* So how's it going?

JULIE: Tommy Sanders asked me to Homecoming.

KIRSTEN: You're kidding.

AMANDA: Stop right there. Kirsten, if you start squealing and rolling your eyes I swear I'll kill you.

JULIE: What's with her?

AMANDA: I mean it. There's only about four things anybody around here talks about: Homecoming, Sadie Hawkins, Snow Daze and the Prom.

(Melissa enters.)

MELISSA: Hey, Clinton.

CLINTON: Scram.

AMANDA: Like we're not here to get an education or anything, the really important stuff comes down to four primitive mating rituals!

MELISSA: Dad wants you home after school.

CLINTON: Double-scram.

AMANDA: I mean, has any of you even *read Siddhartha?*

JULIE: *What?*

CLINTON: Melissa, you're not even supposed to be here.

MELISSA: And you are? I'll tell Dad.

CLINTON: You could do that. But then what'll you use for a face?

MELISSA: Fine, I'm telling him for sure. Scarecrow.

CLINTON: Vanish!

(Melissa goes.)

AMANDA: I don't care. Talk about dating the quarterback all you like, pick out your damn dresses, rat your hair and spray it with shellac, just not when I'm anywhere within four hundred yards. Or I. Shall. Scream.

(Silence for a moment.)

JULIE: She reads too much.

KIRSTEN: You are going to the Homecoming Dance with the quarterback? I can't believe it!

AMANDA: Get me out of here.

JULIE: I didn't tell him yes yet.

KIRSTEN: What? Are you out of your mind?

JULIE: Who knows? Maybe Clinton's gonna ask me.

CLINTON: Get me out of here.

DAVIS: I vote we make the trumpeter president of our club.

AMANDA: I hate that word, "club." And this better not be like where you vote on things and make motions and second them or I'm quitting.

DAN: Probably he's a total jerk.

DAVIS: I don't mean we ever need to meet him, I just want him for president, he's so brilliant.

AMANDA: That's fine, cause she doesn't want to meet you either.

DAVIS: President *ex temporaneous.*

DAN: I mean, that's all he ever does—doesn't he ever go to class?

KIRSTEN: Oh, my god, I'm late for my third period!

AMANDA: I warned you, Kirsten, you shoulda been on the pill.

KIRSTEN: *(gathering up her books)* I don't even know what you're talking about half the time.

(Kirsten goes; Harley enters.)

DAVIS: Hi.

JULIE: Hi, Harley.

CLINTON: So what'd he do, Harley, what'd he say?

HARLEY: *(to Jake)* Gimme a Coke.

AMANDA: *(to Davis)* You coming to history?

DAVIS: In a minute.

AMANDA: *(Gathering up her books.)* I gotta go.

HARLEY: You gotta go?

AMANDA: I think that's what I said.

HARLEY: You want a Coke?

AMANDA: No. Thanks.

HARLEY: You wanna go to Homecoming with me?

AMANDA: *(a shriek)* Aaach! *(Amanda stomps out.)*

CLINTON: Good timing, man. So, you get detention or what?

DAN: Come on, Harley, there are onion rings riding on this.

(Harley suddenly grabs Dan by the hair, yanks his head back.)

DAN: Ow!

DAVIS: Hey. He was rough on you, right?

HARLEY: Come over after?

DAVIS: Sure. I'm really sorry.

(Harley releases Dan.)

HARLEY: No sweat. It's not like you had onion rings riding on it or anything.

(Lights change. The kids disperse, leaving Clinton alone. The trumpet rises, playing the black gospel hymn, "Leaning on the Everlasting Arm.")

3.

Maybe there's a spot on Clinton. He stands at the microphone. Under this we hear the trumpet: "Leaning on the Everlasting Arm."

CLINTON: "I know you are asking today, How long will it take? I come to say to you this afternoon, however difficult the moment, however frustrating the hour, it will not be long, because truth pressed to earth will rise again.

"How long? Not long, because no lie can live forever.

"How long? Not long, because you still reap what you sow.

"How long? Not long. Because the arm of the moral universe is long, but it bends toward justice.

"How long? Not long. 'Cause mine eyes have seen the glory of the coming of the Lord…He has sounded forth the trumpets that shall never call retreat. He is lifting up the hearts of man before His judgment seat. Oh, be swift, my soul, to answer Him. Be jubilant, my feet. Our God is marching on."

(We hear a vast audience responding shouting—applauding. Melissa enters.)

MELISSA: I'm sick of it.

CLINTON: Hey! Respect.

MELISSA: They push and they push. What do they want from us?

CLINTON: You gotta ask?

MELISSA: Don't tell me you don't feel it. You bring home straight A's, anybody else's folks be so happy, they buy you a car. But no…

CLINTON: Shut up now.

MELISSA: "Did you earn this, or did you get by on charm." I'm sick of it!

CLINTON: They're just, you know, doing the best they can.

MELISSA: So am I, dammit! Clinton, it's Homecoming.

CLINTON: Melissa, you are way too young for that old dance.

MELISSA: You aren't. Anyway, there's other things.

CLINTON: If I'd wanted to go, I'da gone.

MELISSA: There's the Pep Rally, maybe I wanted to be there? And all the kids in my class, they're hanging out outside the gym in the parking lot right now, and where am I? Clint, it's Friday night, it's Homecoming and I am at *home,* dammit!

CLINTON: Well you gotta admit, there is a kind of logic...

MELISSA: Don't make fun!

CLINTON: Hey—come on, sweet thing.

MELISSA: We were the only kids at the whole game who had to sit with their parents. Probably we were the only kids whose parents came. I was so embarrassed I wanted to die.

CLINTON: No, you didn't.

(Beat.)

MELISSA: I'm not ever going to get grades like you.

CLINTON: Mellie. Give it time. You gotta work.

MELISSA: I don't want to be a representative of any damn thing!

CLINTON: I know, I know.

MELISSA: I represent me!

CLINTON: I know, honey. *(He holds her.)* And as such, you gotta get that grade-point up.

MELISSA: God, I hate you.

CLINTON: I know.

(Trumpet rises, ceases, lights change.)

4.

Julie and Kirsten lit by the harsh fluorescent light of the girl's bathroom. The two of them, dressed for the Homecoming Dance, stand at the sinks, touching up their makeup in the mirrors. We hear the sound of a record playing over the P.A. system in the school gymnasium, e.g., "Light My Fire."

KIRSTEN: Okay. Okay. What has he said so far? God, he is just so cute. Julie?

JULIE: Wait a minute, willya, I got something in my eye.

KIRSTEN: He must be just so proud.

JULIE: Dammit, what is this thing?

KIRSTEN: And that suit! I thought it was so nice, the way he said hello to me.

JULIE: My eye is killing me.

KIRSTEN: So what has he said to you?

JULIE: When?

KIRSTEN: All night.

JULIE: Since he picked me up? You gotta be kidding.

KIRSTEN: Okay, just some of the things.

JULIE: I don't know, Kirsten, geez. Guys are pretty much the same. You just let 'em babble on. They're only looking at your breasts anyway. *(A moment's shock.)*

KIRSTEN: Not Tommy Sanders. I thought he was such a gentleman, I mean, he didn't have to say anything to me, he's only the quarter-back for goodness sake, but he did, he said he was enjoying the punch very much and he thought I looked wonderful and he wasn't looking at my chest at all and there I was, talking to the man of the hour!

JULIE: Kirsten. Didn't your mother ever, you know, teach you anything?

KIRSTEN: She died.

JULIE: Sorry.

KIRSTEN: Thank you.

JULIE: Anyway. You're nice, you should have a date.

KIRSTEN: Are you kidding, I am Chairman of the Food and Beverage Committee, I am practically run off my feet as it is!

JULIE: Can you see what this is? My eye is gonna go solid bloodshot. *(Kirsten examines Julie's eye.)*

KIRSTEN: And I'm not the only one dancing alone, there's lots of us out there, I think that's almost more fun, did you see Debbie Meyers and me out there? We were cracking up!

JULIE: Ow! I'm tearing up, I'm gonna have do my face all over again.

KIRSTEN: Tommy is definitely the most glamorous person here. He's a hero!

JULIE: Kirsten, we lost the game. We lost the Homecoming game.

KIRSTEN: That wasn't Tommy's fault! The other side just got too many points. And anyway, he scored that touchdown, I thought I was gonna die. The way he ran. Did you hear that crowd go wild or did you hear that crowd go wild?

JULIE: Well he's sure looking to score tonight.

KIRSTEN: What? You didn't say that. You didn't mean that. Do you mean that?

JULIE: Kirsten, please, we've only been in here for about five hours, would you please help me?

KIRSTEN: Wait a minute, I think I…Oh, yeah, there's something in
there. Look up. You mean like, go all the way?

JULIE: I'm begging you.

KIRSTEN: Oh golly. Yeah. Just keep looking up, I think it's coming out.
I think it's. It's an eyelash.

JULIE: Shit! Never ever ever get your makeup from Sears!

(Lights change.)

5.

*Amanda and Dan in a room with a candle. Maybe there's low sitar
music, maybe something like the Beatles' "Within You Without You."*

DAN: So there was this lake we always used to go to, my sisters and me
and my parents, when we were camping up north.

AMANDA: Uh-huh.

DAN: And it was called Tame Fish Lake.

AMANDA: Yeah.

DAN: And it was called Tame Fish Lake because all the fish in it were
tame.

AMANDA: Danny.

DAN: I prefer "Dan," actually.

AMANDA: Is this a joke? 'Cause I don't like jokes.

DAN: No, I swear, it's true!

AMANDA: Right.

DAN: Honest! See, these three old brothers bought this lake, years and
years ago.

AMANDA: You don't *buy* a lake, people don't *buy* lakes.

DAN: These guys did. Come on.

AMANDA: You wanna eat the roach?

DAN: No, you have it.

AMANDA: You can have it.

DAN: No, you have it.

AMANDA: I don't need it.

DAN: You have it.

AMANDA: Really?

DAN: Really.

AMANDA: Honest?

DAN: Really.

(Amanda eats the tiny stub of the marijuana cigarette.)

DAN: So these guys bought this lake when they were young, they were from Oklahoma or somewhere, and they all lived together and they never got married and they lived all alone on this lake and they tamed all the fish in it and then it got to be called Tame Fish Lake and every summer when we were camping north of Brainerd we'd drive over one afternoon to see the fish in Tame Fish Lake.

AMANDA: You are so stoned.

DAN: No, really! It's true. We'd drive up this gravel path about I don't know fourteen miles long and finally you'd come to this tarpaper shack where these three old brothers from Oklahoma or somewhere lived and there was this big bell mounted in this big stone thing down by the shore, it was made of big stones put together with cement or something and if you knocked on the door of the tarpaper hut one or two or three of the old brothers would finally come out and they'd say I guess you're here to see the fish.

AMANDA: You are killing me.

DAN: Good. You believe me, don't you?

AMANDA: Sure, why not.

DAN: Thanks for inviting me over.

AMANDA: So?

DAN: So I guess I'm your Homecoming date.

AMANDA: So one or two or three of the big brothers would come out and say...

DAN: Old brothers. They were old, they weren't big.

AMANDA: God, I am dying.

DAN: Really? 'Cause if you don't like this story, I know lots of others.

AMANDA: So it is just a story, right?

DAN: My stories are true, Amanda. Okay?

AMANDA: Okay, okay. So?

DAN: What?

AMANDA: Tell your damned true story!

DAN: Do you want me to go?

AMANDA: No! I want you to tell your story!

DAN: Do you like me at all?

AMANDA: God, Danny.

DAN: Dan.

AMANDA: Dan. Yes. Okay? Tell the story!

DAN: Which one?

(She moans or falls into helpless laughter, however it strikes her.)

DAN: Oh! Tame Fish Lake! Great! I love that story!

AMANDA: So do I, babe.

DAN: I love you.

AMANDA: Shut up and tell your story.

DAN: I mean it.

AMANDA: So do I.

DAN: You like Davis, don't you. He's an intellectual. Like you.

AMANDA: I am not an...God, why does it all have to come down to crap like that?

DAN: Because it does.

AMANDA: Dan? Don't.

DAN: Okay. Okay. These old guys would look at us like we were from Mars or something, even though they saw us every summer, us and about a thousand other tourists. Then one of them, whichever one it was, he'd sort of shrug, and he'd walk down to the shore where this big bell thing was, made of stone and cement, and he'd reach under and yank on the rope and the bell would ring this deep sound, like *"Bong, Bong, Bong,"* and at first you didn't see anything and my sisters would be saying "Where are the tame fish, where are the tame fish?" and then you'd see a little ripple and then a whole lot of ripples and then dozens and hundreds and thousands of fish would come swimming up to shore and whichever old guy it was, he'd toss out bread crumbs by the handful and the fish would jump and splash and the water would just go crazy and the tame fish would eat every crumb.

(Pause.)

AMANDA: Wow.

DAN: It's on the map and everything. Tame Fish Lake.

(Lights change.)

6.

Night. A riverbank. Harley and Davis enter, Harley carrying a six-pack with two bottles remaining, Harley and Davis each carrying an open beer. They look out over the Mississippi. Eventually they'll sit.

DAVIS: It's hot.

(Harley doesn't respond.)

DAVIS: Happy Homecoming. You drunk yet? Me neither. Maybe a little maybe. Little buzz. Is that a. That's a fire down there on shore, somebody's got a fire going. I think your mother likes me. She's nice, she's funny. I don't think my mom ever used a four-letter word in her life.

HARLEY: Not even, like, shit?

DAVIS: Especially not even like shit.

(Harley considers this.)

HARLEY: What do you guys *talk* about?

DAVIS: I dunno. *(Pause.)* Dad's on the road a lot. She gets depressed. I dunno, if we talk it's. Stuff that's in the paper, what's on TV and why am I watching so much of it, things like that. She reads letters to me from the older kids. We go to Mass together. She doesn't really have any friends.

HARLEY: You were a mistake, right?

DAVIS: What? Oh. I never thought about it.

HARLEY: Get outta here. You're only about a zillion years younger than the other kids in your family and you never thought about it?

DAVIS: No.

HARLEY: I think about things like that a lot. You know, destiny? Like, your dad slipped and bingo! There you are.

DAVIS: Shut up. I don't. I don't think about them doing it.

HARLEY: Well, Davey, they did. Unless there's something about you you're not telling anybody.

(Pause.)

DAVIS: I think I'm beginning to feel it.

HARLEY: You want another?

DAVIS: In a minute. God, it's hot.

HARLEY: If it weren't for my mom I'd be long gone. But she's just too all alone.

DAVIS: Where would you go?

HARLEY: Army, Air Force maybe.

DAVIS: You're out of your frigging mind. Vietnam?

HARLEY: Somebody's got to do it.

DAVIS: Why you?

HARLEY: Why not? Why not you? Forget it, you don't have to worry, you'll be tucked up in some college somewhere.

(They look out over the river.)

HARLEY: Why do you hang out with me?

DAVIS: What? Why shouldn't I?

HARLEY: You got money, you don't get in trouble and your mother never says shit.

DAVIS: I don't have that much money.

HARLEY: Nobody in my family ever graduated from high school.

DAVIS: You're an only child.

HARLEY: My mom didn't, I don't know much about my dad, he was just this thing on the couch, but he sure as hell didn't get through school, my cousins, uncles. If I graduate I'll be the first.

DAVIS: Of course you'll graduate.

HARLEY: How much money you got on you?

DAVIS: I dunno. You want another six-pack?

HARLEY: How much?

DAVIS: What is this? Two or three bucks.

HARLEY: I got fifteen cents in my pocket and that's it. In the whole world, that's all I got.

DAVIS: You wanna climb on down to the river?

HARLEY: You don't know who I am, you won't ever know how I feel.

DAVIS: Come on, screw you. Somebody's got a fire going down there, we could...Harley. We were having a good time here.

HARLEY: I think about her all the time.

DAVIS: This is who? Oh, Mandy, right.

HARLEY: Amanda.

DAVIS: Harley, she didn't go to Homecoming with *anyone*. She's just not into it.

HARLEY: I mean really all the time, if I'm brushing my teeth I wonder if she'd like how I do it. I try to brush better. I try to look, you know, more handsome while I'm brushing. It's like she can always see me, I carry her around in my head. It's hard having her watching me all the time, I can't ever relax, you know? I'm all alone and maybe I start to pick my nose or something and I stop myself, I pretend—I don't know—that I was just grabbing for a mosquito or something. And this is when I'm all alone, there's no one there except for this picture of her in my head, watching me. Davis, I don't hardly fart anymore if I can help it. But she doesn't really see me, not ever, I'm not even there. You like her?

DAVIS: I guess. Sure.

HARLEY: She likes you. She sees you.

DAVIS: Get outta here. Gimme another beer.

HARLEY: So I hang around you trying to figure out how you do all the things you do without even thinking about it.

DAVIS: You're kidding. You're crazy.

HARLEY: I know. Who'd want to act like a little wimp like you?

DAVIS: Screw you.

HARLEY: Pretty soon I'll be carrying my books like a girl.
      (*Davis jumps on Harley, they wrestle for just the moment it takes for Harley to pin Davis to the ground.*)

HARLEY: Davis?

DAVIS: Yeah.

HARLEY: You might be an accident. But you're not a mistake. (*Suddenly Harley rolls off Davis, brushes himself off and heads into the night.*)

DAVIS: Where you going?

HARLEY: Down to the river. Gonna crash me a party.

DAVIS: God. It's kind of late. Harley! Wait up!
      (*Davis turns to us. As he speaks, the table at Jake's Place fills up in the dim light. Only Dan does not sit.*)

DAVIS: We crashed the party on the shore. In my mind's eye these old guys down there, hunkered around the flickering bonfire, were, at the very least, murderers. I suppose now they were undergrads from the University. Anyway they were generous with their beer. When I finally crawled home, praying for a dark house, I saw instead lights on in every room. My mother said, "You have the opportunity to bring your friend up to your level; instead you sink to his." But I went to bed thinking, I'm not a mistake. Nobody had ever told me they loved me before. (*Davis is gone.*)

7. SADIE HAWKINS

Jake's Place. Clinton on the microphone.

CLINTON: "Students! Students. Old Waddle-Butt here. The question has been raised—and it's a good question—it's a decent question—it's a fair question—the question has been raised, 'Who *was*...Sadie Hawkins?' And why do we honor her so. Fair enough. Dan Dwyer, will you for the love of Pete sit down."

DAN: That's really mean, Clint, you know? You can be really mean.

CLINTON: "Principal Waddle-Butt to you, Dwyer. You keep asking for it, you haven't been able to sit down for two months."

DAN: Asking for it!

CLINTON: "My boy, you are either going to have incredible calf and thigh muscles, or you'll have back problems the rest of your life."

AMANDA: Oh, he's got back problems right now.

DAN: *(to Amanda)* Geez. You can be pretty mean, too. And I hated *Siddhartha*.

KIRSTEN: *What?*

AMANDA: Then give me back my book!

DAN: Just kidding! There were a lot of good parts in that book I thought.

AMANDA: Give me back my book!

KIRSTEN: Why do you guys always leave me out of everything! That's really not nice!

AMANDA: Oh, shut up, you dip!

(Clinton has planted his legs wide in the manner of a stout person. He holds his arms straight out and claps, in the manner of a seal.)

CLINTON: "People! People!"

JULIE: Look, he's doing it!

(Harley and Davis enter.)

CLINTON: *(Clapping his hands.)* "People? Let there be no more of this! People?"

HARLEY: Throw him a fish.

THE OTHERS: *(overlapping, they're familiar with the phrase)* Throw him a fish!

CLINTON: "I heard that, Harley. You will report to the faculty parking lot at exactly O-nine hundred hours where I will personally attach you with a length of chain to the rear bumper of my Buick."

HARLEY: Hi, Amanda.

DAN: "Hi, Amanda."

(Harley knuckles Dan on his head.)

DAN: Ow!

CLINTON: "I will then drive my Buick in an easterly direction until we reach the state of Connecticut, and the grave of Nathan Hale."

HARLEY: *(to Amanda)* What's going on?

AMANDA: I think your fate is being decided, if you're at all interested.

HARLEY: Hey, I'm really interested in fate, you know? Destiny—the whole thing.

AMANDA: Shhh.

CLINTON: "After paying respects to our namesake, I will personally drag you, Harley, on over to the house of Miss Sadie Hawkins, Nathan Hale's first girlfriend."

(Melissa enters.)

MELISSA: Clinton? Clinton.

CLINTON: "The pushiest girl in Revolutionary history, and the oldest woman on earth."

MELISSA: Dad found out a white girl's taking you to the dance and is he pissed?

(Pause.)

HARLEY: So who is it, Clint?

(Beat.)

CLINTON: "Miss Hawkins will feed us coffee and cake and will tell you about her first date with Nathan Hale and how much better it would be for you to date a *girl* for a change instead of always Davis."

AMANDA: Clint.

HARLEY: Hey.

DAVIS: Clinton.

(Clinton steps down from the mike.)

CLINTON: You've had your entertainment. *(To Melissa)* He "found out?" Get away from me.

MELISSA: Well he asked!

(Clinton heads out.)

HARLEY: Hey.

CLINTON: Is anyone else enrolled here, or am I the only one who's about to go into midterms?

HARLEY: Hey, asshole!

CLINTON: Don't you get it, Harley? I'm just the entertainment, I grin, I dance, you laugh.

(Clinton goes. Lights change, everyone disperses but Davis and Dan.)

8.

Night. Davis and Dan in Jake's Place. The unseen trumpeter plays...Or maybe it's recorded rock music from dance across street.

DAN: I hate Charles Dickens, I hate Pip, he turns out to be such a little jerk. He turns his back on everybody who was ever nice to him and pretends he doesn't know them and he makes a total ass out of himself over this stuck-up bitch who could care less.

DAVIS: That's what makes the story.

DAN: You're kidding. You're saying if Pip were a cool guy who didn't make you throw up there wouldn't be a story?

DAVIS: That's right.

DAN: And *Great Expectations* wouldn't be this supposedly great book.

DAVIS: Right.

DAN: Well that's just such bull.

DAVIS: You want me to help you with your paper or not?

DAN: Wait a minute, wait a minute. What about James Bond? Huh? He's really cool always, he's great. Now those are great books, tell me they aren't great books. And they make great movies. That *Great Expectations* movie they showed us, half the class was asleep, they shoulda called it *No Expectations* .

DAVIS: Let's see your first paragraph.

DAN: Or, *Great Naps.*

DAVIS: Come on.

DAN: Or, *I Got Drool On My Shoulder From Watching Little Pip.*

DAVIS: You're pretty good, you know?

DAN: Or, *Great Expectorations.*

DAVIS: You're really bright, Dan, do you know that?

DAN: Why is everyone in love with Amanda but you?
      (Beat.)

DAVIS: I thought you wanted me to help you.

DAN: I do, that's why I'm asking.

DAVIS: I'm gonna take off.

DAN: Hey, man, don't get mad.

DAVIS: I suppose they're still dancing over there.

DAN: I'm just, you know, interested.

DAVIS: And that lunatic on the trumpet—where is he? Who is he? What does he want?

DAN: So do you—you know—like to wear dresses or something?

DAVIS: What! Fuck you! No! Clinton is full of it!

DAN: Okay, okay…

DAVIS: Dresses? Are you crazy? No!

DAN: Okay, all I know is nothing, you know—what I hear my dad saying.

DAVIS: Here's an idea, okay? Why don't you write about this high school junior who acted like a jerk to anyone who was ever nice to him and made an asshole of himself over some girl who could care less. *(Davis takes his books and leaves.)*

DAN: I was just asking.

9.

Clinton emerges from a side door of the school gymnasium, followed by Julie. As they come out we hear a blast of dance music: something like "I Think We're Alone Now." They sit on a flight of steps. They're dressed for a Sadie Hawkins Day dance. Julie has gone all out with a sort of "Daisy Mae" hillbilly costume, big painted on freckles, and so forth. It's flamboyant, low-cut and sexy compared to Clinton's sober black suit. From inside the school gymnasium, we hear from time to time music of the era, evocative of songs like "Louie Louie." and by the end of the scene, "A Whiter Shade of Pale."

CLINTON: I can't go back in there.

JULIE: You're crazy, no one was looking at you.

CLINTON: This is such a mistake.

JULIE: I think you look fine.

CLINTON: Red flannel shirts and bib overalls.

JULIE: You look like your mother dressed you up for church, I think it's cute.

CLINTON: Oh, god, this is such a mistake.

JULIE: You're like—the country preacher.

CLINTON: Great. You look like. I don't know what you look like.

JULIE: Well thanks a heap.

CLINTON: Daisy Mae.

JULIE: That's what I'm *supposed* to look like, that's what I spent six hours making myself look like.

CLINTON: Well it worked.

JULIE: It's a hillbilly theme.

CLINTON: You're not kidding. You planned this, didn't you. How long were you planning this?

JULIE: Clinton, do you think you could relax for once in your life?

CLINTON: There's a quarterback in there who took you to Homecoming and tonight I'm your date, you want me to relax?

JULIE: You worry too much.

CLINTON: I don't worry half enough.

JULIE: Tommy Sanders is a muscle-bound creep.

CLINTON: Exactly!

(Davis enters, carrying books.)

DAVIS: Hey, Julie. Clint.

JULIE: Hey, Davis. What's going on?

DAVIS: Oh, you know. Nothing. You seen Harley?

CLINTON: You planning on doing a lot of reading tonight, Davis?

DAVIS: Oh. No. I just, you know, carry them. You look great, Julie.

JULIE: Thanks.

DAVIS: Really.

JULIE: Thanks.

DAVIS: So you haven't seen him around, right?

JULIE: Uh-uh.

DAVIS: *(to Clinton)* Did you just come from church or something?

CLINTON: Thanks a lot, Davis. Goodnight, Davis.

DAVIS: Right.

(Davis goes.)

CLINTON: You cold? It's cold.

JULIE: I'm okay.

CLINTON: I mean, your thing, your dress, I was thinking you might be cold.

JULIE: You think it's too revealing?

CLINTON: No. No. I just thought you might be…My father did.

JULIE: What?

CLINTON: Thought your thing, your dress…

JULIE: God, really? How could you tell? He hardly said two words.

CLINTON: That's how I could tell.

JULIE: Well I'm sorry if I made a bad impression.

CLINTON: No. No. That's just him. I think you look fine. And this is…My Mom *did* dress me, can you believe it?

(Julie kisses him. Clinton responds, then pulls back.)

CLINTON: We just can't.

JULIE: Like my freckles?

CLINTON: Julie.

JULIE: They're eyebrow pencil. See?

CLINTON: Julie.

JULIE: They go all the way down.

CLINTON: Don't.

JULIE: I like you, Clinton, is that so very wrong?

CLINTON: You sound like a country-western song.

(Beat)

JULIE: That wasn't very nice.

CLINTON: Please. I like you, too, Julie.

JULIE: Really?

CLINTON: Yes.

JULIE: It's funny. I believe you. When Tommy Sanders said stuff like that, I guess I just *wanted* to believe it. Why don't you have a driver's license?

CLINTON: I do. He just doesn't let me drive.

JULIE: You're kidding. That's kind of crazy.

CLINTON: Well you know. He needs his car. Veterinarians get called out anytime, day or night.

JULIE: He doesn't *let* you?

CLINTON: I drive, I drive. He wants me to succeed. "Kids in cars, they don't amount to a damn thing."

JULIE: At what?

CLINTON: What?

JULIE: Succeed at what?

CLINTON: Good question. Being a Negro.

JULIE: God—really?

CLINTON: Oh, yeah, it's a riot, isn't it. Right now half the kids in that gym are ready to kill me, maybe you didn't notice.

JULIE: I'm not stupid.

CLINTON: The jocks, the white ones, they're about to send out for rope. The black guys look at me and then they look at you in that…thing, and then they look at me again. And the black chicks? They won't bother with rope, they'll take me apart with their bare hands.

JULIE: At least they care about you.

CLINTON: What are. You talking. About.

JULIE: Your parents, they care.

CLINTON: Julie, you have an interesting mind.

JULIE: My mother, I'm lucky if she looks up when I walk in the room.

CLINTON: Maybe when you're changing the subject you could hold up one finger.

JULIE: I'm talking to you! I'm trying to talk to you.

CLINTON: Sorry.

JULIE: My mother, the biggest favor I could do for her is disappear. I know what the boys say about me, I know what Tommy Sanders has been saying ever since Homecoming.

CLINTON: I don't hang out with those guys.

JULIE: But you know how they talk about me. 'Cause everybody says it. You know what they say. Don't you. Don't you.

(Beat.)

CLINTON: Yes.

JULIE: They say I'm easy. Well I'll tell you one thing, Clinton, easy is about the last thing it is.

(Beat.)

CLINTON: It ain't easy all over. Can I take you to Jake's?

JULIE: Now?

CLINTON: Cheeseburger deluxe and a double malt?

JULIE: I guess. Look how I'm dressed!

CLINTON: I think you look great. *(He kisses her—a good one.)*

JULIE: Who's that? There's someone there.

CLINTON: *(finally)* Something bothering you, Harley?

(Harley, quite drunk, emerges from the shadows.)

HARLEY: Means nothing to me.

CLINTON: Good.

HARLEY: Wouldn't go back in that gym though.

CLINTON: Why's that.

(Davis enters, with his books.)

DAVIS: Hey, Harley, where were you, you didn't show up.

CLINTON: Why's that, Harley.

HARLEY: *(to Clinton)* Go anywhere you want, means nothing to me.

JULIE: Let's go.

CLINTON: Julie. Do you think you could…? I'd like to take you back in there and do some dancing.

JULIE: Oh god, why?

CLINTON: Cause I think I have to. Okay?

HARLEY: Seven guys in there just waiting for you. I was just doing you a favor.

JULIE: Clinton?

HARLEY: You go on in, be a hero. It means nothing to me. *(To Davis)* Neither do you. *(Harley exits.)*

CLINTON: Damn.

JULIE: Clint.

CLINTON: Damn.

JULIE: I'm a little scared.

CLINTON: We'll go to Jake's, okay! We're going to Jake's! *(Clinton strides off, followed by Julie.)*

JULIE: See ya, Davis.

(Davis stands alone.)

10. SNOW DAZE

DAVIS: *(to us)* By the end of 1967, there were 486,000 American troops in Vietnam, a disproportionate number of them poor and black. Nearly 10,000 died there that year. In October, a hundred and fifty thousand protesters marched on the Pentagon. A few of them stuck blossoms into the barrels of the soldiers' rifles. Hundreds were arrested.

The race riots of the long hot summer had cooled some, but over a hundred American cities had burned and there was nobody to haul away the ashes.

In January, North Vietnam launched the Tet offensive, and the Green Bay Packers beat Oakland in Super Bowl II. Like I cared.

I was working on the big stuff.

(Kirsten passes, with books, on her way to Jake's Place.)

DAVIS: Kirsten?

KIRSTEN: Hi.

DAVIS: Would you go to Snow Daze with me?

KIRSTEN: What?

DAVIS: Snow Daze. The dance.

KIRSTEN: I guess. Really? Sure. Me? Thanks. Yes. Thanks. Oh, wow.
(Kirsten goes, sits at a table with Amanda. Davis steps into a confessional and kneels. After a moment, Clinton enters and kneels on the opposite side of the screen.)
DAVIS: Father, forgive me, for I have sinned.
CLINTON: How long has it been since your last confession?
DAVIS: Look—can I just skip to what I want to say? My mother's got me going to this shrink because she's afraid maybe I'm not normal. Okay, me too, maybe I'm afraid I'm maybe not normal. But I hate it! This old guy with hairs growing out of his nose and his ears, he keeps talking about his own childhood, like how hard he had it, sole support of about 28 brothers and sisters, and I don't really care, you know? And about healthy thoughts and unhealthy thoughts, but Father, I hate it, I don't feel sick. I don't think I'm sick, I don't know. If I were sick, wouldn't I feel sick? I sort of want to clip the hairs on the end of his nose, maybe that's sick. But I've asked this girl to the next dance you know, and that scares me a little bit. So what I want to know is about the power of prayer and all that. You know?
(Pause.)
CLINTON: Are you a homosexual? *(Silence.)* Keep going to the shrink.
(Clinton leaves, Davis stands.)
DAVIS: Wow, was that a good idea!
(Harley crosses wearing heavy parka, carrying a massive shopping bag and packages.)
HARLEY: You do that a lot? Go to church and all?
DAVIS: How've you been?
HARLEY: Oh, you know. Hey, you want a salad bowl or anything?
DAVIS: What?
(Harley pulls a large box from the shopping bag.)
HARLEY: *(reading the package)* "Salad bowl and tongs, genuine teak." You want it?
DAVIS: I don't get it.
HARLEY: It's free, I mean, it's for you. Merry Christmas.
DAVIS: Well. Thanks. Where'd you get it?
HARLEY: I been Christmas shopping.
DAVIS: Well. That's really nice. Thanks. I don't have anything for you, at least not yet.
HARLEY: Forget it.

DAVIS: I didn't know if, you know. I just haven't seen much of you for a while. I'm going to Snow Daze.

HARLEY: No shit.

DAVIS: Really.

HARLEY: With her?

DAVIS: Who? Oh, Mandy. No.

HARLEY: Amanda.

DAVIS: With Kirsten, I asked her.

HARLEY: Who?

DAVIS: Kirsten Sabo.

HARLEY: Oh yeah. Great. Davis?

DAVIS: Yeah?

HARLEY: Listen, you know, I was bombed that night, Sadie Hawkins, I don't even remember it.

DAVIS: Forget it.

HARLEY: I want you to have this. *(Harley pulls a small box from his bag, gives it to Davis.)*

DAVIS: No. Uh-uh. Thanks, I can't. Where did you get this?

HARLEY: Take it. It's fourteen jewels, it's a Bulova.

DAVIS: Harley, what's going on?

HARLEY: You're still the only guy I can talk to. Who listens to me. You respect me, you don't make me feel small.

DAVIS: You're not getting into trouble, are you Harley?

HARLEY: No, I had good luck. I got the watch and a Barlow knife and a hair dryer for my mom and. Look at this. *(He pulls another box from the bag.)* It's a Bell & Howell!

DAVIS: Oh, god, Harley.

HARLEY: I know, it's great, a movie camera!

DAVIS: I can't keep this watch.
    (Beat.)

HARLEY: Look, you do your shopping in stores, I do mine in the parking ramp.

DAVIS: Oh, shit. Harley?

HARLEY: Davey. What means more? You got money, you put it on a counter, you give somebody a present. Me, I had to risk everything to give you that stuff. Ask yourself.
    (Pause.)

DAVIS: No more, don't do it anymore. Okay?
    (Harley tucks the small box containing the watch in Davis's pocket.)

HARLEY: No sweat, I always get my Christmas shopping done in a day. I'll see ya, Davis.

(Harley leaves. Davis goes to Jake's Place. As he enters, Kirsten gets up from her table, leaving only Amanda there with a cup of coffee.)

KIRSTEN: *(to Amanda)* See ya! *(to Davis)* See ya, Davis. *(Kirsten goes.)*

DAVIS: Hi. Hey, you're reading *The Lord of the Rings*.

(She doesn't respond.)

DAVIS: I loved it. Where are you? *Two Towers.* Great.

AMANDA: What's that?

DAVIS: Um. A salad bowl.

AMANDA: I guess we've known each other since what? Junior high?

DAVIS: I guess, yeah.

AMANDA: I remember precisely. You were probably the skinniest thirteen-year-old I'd ever seen. We used to share books, or we'd read them at the same time and enthuse together.

DAVIS: You want some more coffee or something?

AMANDA: You don't have to do that.

DAVIS: It's nothing, let me get you a cup of coffee.

AMANDA: I mean you don't have to run away, you don't have to get all nervous, you never used to. We used to talk for hours.

DAVIS: I'm not nervous.

(Beat.)

AMANDA: Here was this 13-year-old doing a pretty good imitation of a drinking straw with legs, and your shirt always out of the back of your pants and you always carried about 48 books with you wherever you went.

DAVIS: Oh god. Still do.

AMANDA: Still do. Always enough books to cover anything that could conceivably arise in a given class, plus about ten others of no conceivable use.

DAVIS: What a dip.

AMANDA: Not to me. *(Beat.)* My parents were going to put me in a private school this year. Very exclusive.

DAVIS: Yeah?

AMANDA: I said no.

DAVIS: Yeah?

AMANDA: Yeah. That's what I said. No. So you're going to dances now, huh?

DAVIS: Well, this one, yeah.

AMANDA: With Kirsten.

DAVIS: Well, I asked her, yeah.

(Amanda puts a bookmark in her book.)

AMANDA: I hope you have a good time.

DAVIS: Mandy, you don't go to dances.

AMANDA: No, I don't.

DAVIS: You mean, you would've if I'd asked you? Cause I would've. I mean I just wanted a girl to go with, it didn't matter who and I'd much rather go with you.

AMANDA: While you're thinking about what you just said, I'll be telling myself that you're just a late bloomer. *(Amanda takes her books and goes.)*

DAVIS: *(to us)* On a lighter note. You carry your books in front of you, you're a girl, everyone knows that. You carry them under one arm at your side, you're a guy. Like she said, I always had about 48 books to haul from one class to the other. But once I got put in the picture, I always carried those 48 books under one arm, at my side, in the prescribed fashion. With the result that my passage down any hall was forever punctuated by the thud of falling books. Here comes Davis!

I was working on all of it. The country was burning, kids my age were dying in Asia but I was working very hard on the important things. I don't mean to say I was alone in this. Far from it.

11.

Julie and Melissa practicing a line dance of the era. They keep dancing—either to music or to no music throughout the scene.

MELISSA: I hate my face.

JULIE: Your face is fine, everybody hates their face. I hate my hair.

MELISSA: It's all, I don't know, flat or something.

JULIE: Is something wrong with Clinton?

MELISSA: What *isn't* wrong with Clinton?

JULIE: He just seems sort of different.

MELISSA: He *is* sort of different.

JULIE: No, I mean lately.

MELISSA: Oh. Lately.

JULIE: Like he's changed.

MELISSA: Oh, yeah. Elijah Muhammed.

JULIE: What *is* all that stuff?

MELISSA: *I* don't know. Dad's really pissed, but Clint keeps
going to the meetings. I hate my hair, too.

JULIE: I hate my nails. I don't think I've ever had all ten of them at one
time ever.

MELISSA: Me neither.

JULIE: They take turns. If they'd all break at once, you could just start
over, you know?

MELISSA: I know.

JULIE: I think maybe your parents are starting to like me.

MELISSA: Oh, no, they hate you.

JULIE: Oh god, really?

MELISSA: I mean, not you, the idea of you. They like you personally, I
can tell, they think you're really cute and really nice. I mean, you
know, it would just help a lot if you were black. And you gotta get
that grade-point up.

(They continue to dance.)

JULIE: I hate my teeth.

MELISSA: I hate my ears.

(Lights change, distant rock music.)

12.

*Kirsten sits on a staircase in the school. From down the hall we hear
music over the gymnasium P.A. system, maybe something on the order
of a Chuck Berry number, e.g., "Rock & Roll Music" or "School Days"
or perhaps the Stones' "Under the Boardwalk," and then something like
the Beatles' "She's Leaving Home." Davis approaches with hot cider in
Dixie cups.*

KIRSTEN: Oh, thanks!

DAVIS: Look out, they're hot.

KIRSTEN: Steaming. It's my Dad's recipe multiplied by a couple hundred.
Heavy on the cinnamon.

DAVIS: It smells great.

KIRSTEN: Thank you. I made the fruit salad, too. You're a wonderful dancer.

DAVIS: Thanks, I'm not that...

KIRSTEN: I mean, you never go to dances, where did you learn to dance like that?

DAVIS: I don't know.

KIRSTEN: You're just amazing.

DAVIS: You tired or anything?

   (Beat.)

KIRSTEN: My dad helps me with so much, he's such a great guy, I mean, he's a little quiet, he's a mailman.

DAVIS: Uh-huh.

KIRSTEN: They tend to be quiet, letter carriers, they think a lot, I don't think people generally realize that.

   (Beat.)

DAVIS: And walk, they walk a lot.

KIRSTEN: Oh, yes. Walk and think, think and walk.

DAVIS: Really. Is there, you know, wax or something floating in your cider?

KIRSTEN: Oh, no, I just knew it! I knew Dixie cups were a mistake!

DAVIS: I mean, it's not a lot or anything.

KIRSTEN: Miss Borders said she didn't think it would be a problem and I said, "Oh yes it will, you just wait."

DAVIS: It's only a little wax.

KIRSTEN: That woman just doesn't listen. Sorry, I shouldn't criticize.

DAVIS: Why not?

KIRSTEN: Well. It's like Thumper's dad was always saying to him, "If you can't say somethin' nice, don't say nothin' at all."

DAVIS: Thumper's dad?

KIRSTEN: In *Bambi.* The movie?

DAVIS: Oh, yeah.

KIRSTEN: It was my favorite movie when I was a kid. Remember it?

DAVIS: Yeah, I think so.

KIRSTEN: If you want to go, Davis, I'll understand.

DAVIS: What?

KIRSTEN: I know you're thinking this was a mistake.

DAVIS: No! Honest. No.

KIRSTEN: You're a kind person, you always have been. But I'll understand.

DAVIS: Hey, I don't know what you're talking about, really. I'm having a great time.

KIRSTEN: You're really so sweet. But you sure as hell don't have a crush on me.

(Beat.)

DAVIS: I don't think I ever heard you use a four-letter word before.

KIRSTEN: I'm never going to win a Nobel Prize or anything, but I'm not a damn fool.

DAVIS: Wow.

KIRSTEN: Girls. I don't know, they're different. They get crushes.

DAVIS: Boys do too.

(Beat.)

KIRSTEN: And I'm not kidding, I think the two of you would be so perfect.

DAVIS: Who?

KIRSTEN: You and Amanda.

DAVIS: Oh, god!

KIRSTEN: Let's go.

DAVIS: No! Kirsten. Please. Let's go back in there and dance some more. Or we could stay here if you like. Talk to me.

(Pause.)

KIRSTEN: My dad was so nervous tonight, you'd think he was the one going on a. To the dance. And a little proud, too, I think, you know? But mostly just nervous. He felt better when he met you, I could tell. Did he give you the old third degree while I was upstairs?

DAVIS: No. He didn't say much really.

KIRSTEN: Oh.

DAVIS: I mean, we talked. He gave me a Coke. Mostly he read the paper.

KIRSTEN: I think my dad's a lot more like Thumper's dad than Bambi's dad. Of course Bambi's dad was a great big stag and the King of the Forest and my dad's a lot more like an old rabbit. Bambi's mom died around the same time mine did, I mean, that's about when I saw that movie, right round the time my mom died, and we both missed our moms terribly. I think of all the things I should have said to her but didn't. I guess that's why you mourn. Then you go on. Like Bambi did. This is the first time I ever went out with a boy.

I think my dad was afraid I was going to get all twitter-pated tonight and that's why he was so nervous.

DAVIS: Twitter-pated?

KIRSTEN: You'll have to see the movie. At Luther League at church they pair you off for parties or hayrides but that's different. A boy tried to kiss me once on a hayride but I didn't like him so I didn't let him. There was one boy at church I sort of liked but he moved.

(Beat.)

DAVIS: Should I kiss you?

KIRSTEN: I don't know.

(Davis kisses Kirsten.)

KIRSTEN: It's not Amanda? I won't ask. When I talk to myself I sound interesting but when I say things out loud I don't.

DAVIS: I'm interested.

KIRSTEN: And that's a real problem because what you say out loud is important, it's like a bridge, and if you don't have it you're all alone. So whatever you've got to say, Davis, whoever you've got to say it to, you better say it. I would like to go to the girls' room now. *(She starts off and turns back.)* Let me take these, they're undrinkable.

(Kirsten takes Davis's Dixie cup and her own and leaves. Maybe Davis puts his head in his arms.)

13. THE PROM

Continuous action, but several weeks later. After a moment, Clinton enters and sits beside Davis.

CLINTON: Saw you at Snow Daze with Kirsten. You're making progress, man.

DAVIS: Screw you. Saw you there with Julie, you didn't even start one riot, you're slipping.

CLINTON: Double-screw to you. I think I'm going to be a doctor.

DAVIS: Great, can I make an appointment?

CLINTON: You okay?

DAVIS: Not a shrink, right?

CLINTON: Not a shrink, I think maybe internal…What's wrong with you?

DAVIS: You're talking to white folks these days?

(Beat.)

CLINTON: You don't count.

DAVIS: You hardly ever come into Jake's anymore, you never want to hang out. We used to hang out, Clint. The Less Than Human Club barely exists without you. You still going with Julie?

CLINTON: Is the Pope arthritic?

DAVIS: I thought you really liked her.

CLINTON: Who said I didn't like her?

DAVIS: Fine.

(Beat.)

CLINTON: My dad drilled it into us, aim high, aim high, Melissa and me, aim high. Now I tell him I want to go into pre-med, he's furious, you know why? That's too high. Be a vet like me. Is that perfect? From the time I was twelve, he had me memorizing Martin Luther King's speeches, and Davis I am telling you, that man is a fine speaker but he does go on. Mom stepped in on that one, thank God, it's just excerpts now, can you believe it? They won't hardly talk to Julie. Know why? Aimed too low there. See, it's a fine line. That's a human being they're calling low. That's my girl they're calling low. So I start doing some thinking on my own, right? Read up on Elijah Muhammed, there's a group in the city meets once a week. Muslims, Davis, not Lutherans, not Catholics, whatever you are. And at first I think, Cool. This is way beyond M.L. King, Junior. And inside of two months, they're on me and on me and on me for going out with a white girl. So where am I? What do I do?

DAVIS: I don't know.

CLINTON: I'm thinking, Fuck 'em all. I'm thinking, I'm on my own.

DAVIS: I'm gonna be late for history.

CLINTON: You're not kidding, history is leaving you behind. You know who you are?

DAVIS: I know you think you know who I am.

CLINTON: You're the person people talk to. You really pull it off, too, you know—nobody even notices you hardly ever say a word yourself. They talk, they spill their guts, and they go away thinking they had a conversation with you. Go to history.

DAVIS: Give me a break, I've got a class.

CLINTON: Why aren't we better friends? There're times I think, shit, he's the only person here I *could* talk to, but you won't talk back so what's the point.

DAVIS: We're friends.

CLINTON: Evasion! God you're good at that. Duck and weave, like Muhammed Ali. You could be a boxer. You could be a spy, you never give away a thing.

DAVIS: I don't know what you're talking about.

CLINTON: So you've got this crummy little secret, who gives a damn!

DAVIS: Watch out Clint, I mean it.

CLINTON: Don't you see? We're both outsiders, we could be allies, only I can't hide who I am.

DAVIS: Who are you?

CLINTON: I asked you first.

DAVIS: So you tell me.

CLINTON: Oh go to history.

DAVIS: I could use an ally.

(*Clinton is leaving.*)

DAVIS: Clint.

CLINTON: History was made for liars.

(*Clinton goes, Amanda enters.*)

14.

Continuous, but it's several weeks later: Amanda and Davis.

AMANDA: You on your way to algebra?

DAVIS: Yeah.

AMANDA: I just wanted you to know, I'm transferring out at the end of the year.

DAVIS: You're kidding.

AMANDA: I don't think so. I'll be going to St. John's in the fall.

DAVIS: Wow. That's a good school.

AMANDA: Yes. So.

DAVIS: I guess, you know. Congratulations.

AMANDA: Yeah. So. We've only got a few months left.

DAVIS: Three.

AMANDA: Two-and-a-half. So, I hope we can spend a little time…

DAVIS: *(overlapping)* Oh yeah, definitely.

AMANDA: …make the most of it.

DAVIS: Definitely.

AMANDA: Okay. You coming to class?

DAVIS: In a second. Gotta pee.

AMANDA: Oh. I may go to Europe this summer.

DAVIS: Wow. Europe.

AMANDA: My parents are splitting up so they're feeling really guilty.

DAVIS: Well. Europe sounds good. We'll do something, okay?

AMANDA: Okay.

> *(Amanda leaves, Davis goes to Boy's Room.—No doors, no break in action, but it's weeks later.)*

15.

> *Dan is already in the Boy's Room. Perhaps he's leaning over a sink. He's clearly not well.*

DAVIS: Hey Dwyer.

> *(Dan does not respond. Davis goes toward a urinal, then goes back to Dan.)*

DAVIS: You okay? You want to talk?

DAN: I think I could kill him. Davis? Do you think you could take a look at my butt? I think there's blood down there.

DAVIS: Goddamn. Goddamned sadist. You gotta tell somebody, Dan.

DAN: No! No.

DAVIS: Then I will.

DAN: You can't! No! Promise you won't.

DAVIS: Why not?

DAN: Cause then he'll win.

DAVIS: This is crazy. You gotta go to the nurse.

DAN: Next year I won't have him, seniors don't get Knipsy. I'm just scared to look at it, could you look at it?

DAVIS: Oh, no, man. Go to the nurse.

> *(Dan unbuckles his belt and lowers his pants just a bit.)*

DAVIS: Christ.

DAN: Oh, no.

DAVIS: It's okay, there's some blood, it's gonna be okay but you gotta go to the nurse's office, okay?

DAN: Is it on my shorts?

DAVIS: Yeah.

DAN: Damn! What am I gonna tell my mom?

DAVIS: Tell her what he did to you, dammit.

DAN: I'll put 'em in the garbage, she'll never see.

DAVIS: Tell somebody.

(Dan buckles up his pants.)

DAN: You really don't understand.

DAVIS: No I sure don't. Why do you let him do it?

DAN: What am I gonna do? He's the teacher, it's his job. He's bigger than me. Anyway, it used to be kind of funny. There's a kind of glory in it, to be singled out like that. Nobody gets the lanyard more than me. By now everybody expects me to get it, and I do. Everybody's waiting to see if I'll cry, everybody talks about my welts, they say "Hey, did you see the stripes on Dan's butt, they came up a quarter of an inch yesterday." I'm famous. God, I feel sick.

DAVIS: I'll take you to the nurse, okay?

DAN: It's okay, I'll go. I'll tell her I just need to lie down for a while. I've done it before, she just says "There's the cot." I'll be okay. *(Dan pulls himself together to leave.)* Davis?

DAVIS: Yeah.

DAN: Don't tell anybody I was crying, okay?

(Dan goes. Davis goes to Jake's Place.)

16.

Davis sits at a table. Harley enters and sits with him. The trumpeter plays something like a solo version of "Goin' Out of My Head."

HARLEY: I'm going nuts here. This place is killing me. You gotta help me, Davey. You gotta go to her, she likes you, she respects you, you gotta see if I stand a chance here.

DAVIS: Oh, geez, Harley.

HARLEY: Will you do it? I want to ask her to the Prom, you know? And if she's gonna, you know, vomit or something, I'd just as soon not ask her. So that's where I am. You gonna help me?

DAVIS: Shit.

HARLEY: You're the only one I could ever count on. If she says no, you know, then I'll know.

DAVIS: Dammit, Harley.

HARLEY: You're wearing my watch.

DAVIS: Yeah. The salad bowl didn't fit on my wrist.

HARLEY: Huh?

DAVIS: I'll do it, dammit! Okay? And if she says no, you're okay, right? Promise?

HARLEY: I'll get her out of my head anyway. I'll be free. I'll be free.

(We hear the sound of a distant gunshot, and the trumpet is suddenly silent. Almost immediately Clinton runs on.)

CLINTON: They shot him. They shot him. They killed him.

(Lights slowly change during the following, ending in spot on Clinton. Meanwhile, all the others enter and sit.)

CLINTON: They shot him in Memphis. He was on the balcony. Where's that goddamn microphone? *(Clinton runs to mike, grabs it.)* Listen! Everybody! shit. *(Clinton switches on the mike, loud feedback noises.)* Listen! Listen! They killed Martin! They shot Martin! Shit! Goddamn this thing! *(He bangs on the mike, the feedback squeals get louder.)* They killed Martin! They killed Martin! Listen! Listen! *(Spot on Clinton. Feedback squeals deafening. Julie takes him away. Spot on mike, feedback noises fading. Spot off, blackout.)*

17.

Amanda and Davis at the zoo, looking at the giant baboons.

AMANDA: They're so big.

DAVIS: They're so slow.

AMANDA: They're so playful, they're so human.

DAVIS: They know how to have a good time. Eeww, don't look.

AMANDA: Stop. See how they take care of each other?

DAVIS: Mandy? You got a couple lice crawling up your neck here…

AMANDA: Yeah, what of it?

DAVIS: ...you want me to pick 'em off with my fingers or my teeth?

AMANDA: Ooo! Be still my heart!

DAVIS: It's great, they pick off the lice or whatever that is, they look at it for a minute, then they pop it in their mouth and eat it. Nothing is wasted.

AMANDA: You've really got a thing for the grotesque, don't you.

DAVIS: I beg your pardon.

AMANDA: I mean who else would spend an hour and a half with the Equatorial Insects?

DAVIS: You said you loved that exhibit!

AMANDA: Hated it. I only said that because you were so clearly loving those creepy things.

DAVIS: I was terrified of those creepy things! I loathe spiders! Especially the kind with fur.

AMANDA: Oh no.

DAVIS: I hate any living creature that has more than a decent number of legs. I kept wondering, what does she see in all this? Why does she linger?

AMANDA: You're kidding.

DAVIS: I was praying all the time: Oh, Lord, let her get tired of the bugs!

AMANDA: Oh, that's perfect. I thought, well, maybe it's his thing.

DAVIS: We could have been with the baboons all that time! I was thinking, this woman is less than human!

AMANDA: *(overlapping)* Less than human! I have loved this whole day.

DAVIS: Me too.

AMANDA: Despite your peculiarities.

DAVIS: Hey—there's a whole patch of 'em in your hair.

AMANDA: Shut up!

(Davis is close to her, examining her hair.)

DAVIS: It's. It's the Lice Family!

AMANDA: Shut...

DAVIS: It's the Lice Family Singers!

AMANDA: Oh I hate you so much.

DAVIS: I. I think they're dancing.

(Somehow they kiss. They're both surprised.)

DAVIS: *(finally, singing)* "Edelweis, Edelweis..."

(Maybe Amanda slugs him.)

AMANDA: I'm gonna miss you.

DAVIS: I'll miss you, too.

AMANDA: And everybody. Even Kirsten. Oh! Hey, I didn't mean…

DAVIS: It's okay, I know what you mean.

AMANDA: She's sweet, she really is.

DAVIS: She is.

AMANDA: Really. I just mean. I'm even gonna miss Harley.

DAVIS: You know he's crazy about you.

AMANDA: Well I'm crazy about him, it's fun knowing a real live criminal.

DAVIS: That's not all he is. I think he's gonna ask you to the Prom.

AMANDA: Oh, god, no.

DAVIS: You wouldn't go with him?

AMANDA: You're serious? You're serious. Dammit, Davis, here I was, having a good time.

DAVIS: So it's out of the question.

AMANDA: Until a minute ago I thought I might get a different invitation.

DAVIS: *(finally)* Kirsten said something. She said, "Whatever you've got to say, whoever you've got to say it to, you better say it." I don't. I don't say things, not the real stuff. So, there's only a few people on my list and you're one of them.

AMANDA: Say it.

DAVIS: I'm not gonna be going to any more dances for a while. I'm trying to figure things out, and I just won't be going. But I want you to know, I think you're terrific and…

AMANDA: Shhh.

DAVIS: I mean it.

AMANDA: Be quiet. *(Amanda stares into the baboon pen.)* They're sleeping. *(Lights fade to a low level, Amanda leaves, Davis sits on the ground.)*

18.

Davis sits on the riverbank. Harley joins him with half a six-pack of beer.

DAVIS: Harley?

HARLEY: Yeah.

DAVIS: I believe that whatever a person's got to say, whoever he's got to say it to, he better say it.

HARLEY: You talked to her.

DAVIS: That wasn't what I.

HARLEY: You talked to her, didn't you.

DAVIS: Yeah.

HARLEY: Oh, god. Okay.

DAVIS: Gimme another.

(Harley gives Davis a beer, they each pop one open and drink.)

HARLEY: Okay. Okay. What did she say.

DAVIS: She likes you. She's really, in a way, crazy about you.

HARLEY: No. Oh god, oh god.

DAVIS: Wait a minute, Harley. Geez. *(Davis drinks.)*

HARLEY: So? What?

DAVIS: She's not gonna be going to the Prom with you.

HARLEY: She's not.

DAVIS: No.

HARLEY: Not even if I ask her.

DAVIS: No.

HARLEY: Oh.

DAVIS: Come on, Harley, she really does like you, she told me.

HARLEY: Is it because of, you know, my reputation?

DAVIS: No, no. Now just let it go, okay?

HARLEY: She saw my mom's house once, she was walking by, I came out, I wanted to die. Is it money? Is it cause I live in a place like that?

DAVIS: Don't be stupid.

HARLEY: Sucker, don't you call me stupid!

DAVIS: Screw you. Act stupid and I'll call you stupid.

(Pause.)

HARLEY: I feel like a fool. You didn't come out and ask her, did you, you just sort of sounded her out, right? God, I feel so stupid.

DAVIS: Hey. Buddy. Don't. Don't cry, man, you'll regret it in the morning.

HARLEY: You're okay, Davey. I love you, man. I just feel so dumb, like I thought she would actually go out with. Shit.

DAVIS: Listen. She said. She said she really likes you but she's changing schools at the end of the year and she just doesn't want to start anything, you know? Like it wouldn't be fair, not to you, not to her.

HARLEY: Yeah?

DAVIS: She said. She said she knows how intelligent you are. And that you keep that a closely guarded secret.

HARLEY: No.

DAVIS: She knows it's not easy, coming from a family that's had its problems, that doesn't have a lot of money. She loves how you love your mom and how you're always looking out for her. She respects you. Deep down you're a good person.

HARLEY: Wow. What else?

DAVIS: Get out of here, Harley.

HARLEY: No, I can take this, at least there's a reason, you know? So what else did she say?

(Davis drinks.)

DAVIS: The rest is just little stuff. The line of almost invisible hairs at the nape of your neck and the way they disappear down into your shirt collar. The fuzz on your upper lip.

HARLEY: Fuzz!

DAVIS: Hey, don't blame me! Your hands, and the veins in your hands. The strength of your hands. The way your eyes, the color of your eyes changes in different kinds of light. Your smile. Especially your smile—when it comes it's the best smile on earth.

HARLEY: Incredible!

DAVIS: Oh, yeah. Your butt. Above all, your butt.

HARLEY: Oh wow, I could kiss you, man! *(Harley grabs Davis's face and gives him a smack.)* Fantastic! This is fantastic!

(In the dim light, Amanda and Dan have gone into Jake's Place, Amanda sitting, Dan standing.)

HARLEY: And she will go out with me! She will go to that dance with me!

DAVIS: Harley.

HARLEY: You watch, man.

DAVIS: Harley.

(Lights come up full.)

19.

Continuous: the next day. Either the trumpeter plays the Beatles' "Got to Get You into My Life," or we hear the actual record. Amanda and Dan in Jake's Place, Harley rushes in. Davis observes from a distance.

HARLEY: Hey. Hi.

AMANDA: Hi.

HARLEY: Listen, it's okay. You can go to the Prom with me, all right? I know you're going away, and I understand but we can go to the Prom together, it's okay.

AMANDA: No. Harley?

HARLEY: Really, it is, it's fine with me.

AMANDA: This is how you ask a girl to the Prom?

HARLEY: Just you know, that one dance.

AMANDA: No. It's not fine with me.

HARLEY: But it's all right, *really.*

AMANDA: Harley, I am not going to any dance with you.

HARLEY: Why not?

AMANDA: God. Cause I'm going with Dan. Cause Dan already asked me and I'm going with him.

(Harley is stunned. He can't speak. Eventually he leaves.)

DAN: *(finally)* Wow. Okay.

(Distant gunshot, and the music ceases. Lights begin to fade as Kirsten enters and goes to microphone. Spot up on Kirsten.)

KIRSTEN: *(over P.A.)* Excuse me. I know I'm not supposed to be using this, but. They shot Senator Kennedy. At the Ambassador Hotel. In Los Angeles, California. Somebody shot Bobby. Bobby is dead.

(Spot out, blackout.)

20.

If possible there's a rotating "glitter ball." In any case, we're in the high school gymnasium for the Junior-Senior Prom. Julie and Clinton slow dance to something like "Goin' Out of My Head."

JULIE: I didn't know if you were going to show up.

CLINTON: I said I would.

JULIE: You're kind of late.

CLINTON: I'm here, aren't I?

(Beat.)

JULIE: You sure are. I think they're getting used to us.

CLINTON: Am I supposed to be grateful?

JULIE: I just mean hardly anyone's looking.

CLINTON: God, Julie, listen to yourself.

JULIE: What?

CLINTON: And I don't *want* anyone getting used to me. Not them, not you, not anybody.

JULIE: Clinton, you think too much.

CLINTON: You don't think at all!

(Julie pulls away from him; Clinton tries to pull her back.)

CLINTON: God, I'm sorry, I didn't mean it.

JULIE: I think all the time, I think about you, I think about a lot of things!

CLINTON: I am so sorry, I mean it, there's just so much pressure...I can't do this here, come on, let's get out of here.

JULIE: I came to dance.

CLINTON: Jule...

JULIE: I came to dance with you.

CLINTON: Please.

JULIE: Can't we just relax and have a good time?

CLINTON: No. Not ever. Come on, dammit.

JULIE: No.

CLINTON: Okay. You think your reputation was so bad before we started going out, do you have any idea what it is now?

JULIE: I think I do.

CLINTON: Well doesn't that make you goddamn furious?

JULIE: Maybe you better go.

CLINTON: Fine.

JULIE: Oh, Clint, don't.

CLINTON: People get used to an old pair of shoes, they get used to an old dog, they get used to the colored boy and his white chick. That's what they get used to and I will not have it!

JULIE: I've been sleeping over to my aunt's, on the couch. For months. Ever since my mom found out about you and me. I've heard plenty about what your family thinks about me but you never. You never asked about mine. You want to teach me something, Clinton? You want to teach me about white trash chicks and what they get for going out with colored boys?

(Julie leaves, after a moment Clinton goes off in another direction. Dan and Amanda slow dance on.)

DAN: He's looking at me, isn't he. I can't believe it. First dance I've been to all year, and who's the faculty monitor?

AMANDA: Is that what he hits you with, that plastic thing around his neck?

DAN: God, he wore his whistle! What a total bozo. Well screw him. I got the most gorgeous girl here, and what's he got? Popeye arms.

AMANDA: You're sweet.

DAN: Damn right.

AMANDA: You know, this isn't like a date or anything.

DAN: Of course not. What *is* it like?

(Continuous: boy's bathroom. Davis is leaning over a sink. Kirsten enters.)

KIRSTEN: Davis?

DAVIS: What are you doing in here. Hi.

KIRSTEN: Are you okay?

DAVIS: You're really sweet. This is the boy's bathroom, Kirsten.

KIRSTEN: I know. I've never been in here before.

DAVIS: Right. Why are you in here?

KIRSTEN: Wow. The whole layout's different.

DAVIS: Once again. You put your finger on the major issues of our time. Oh, lord. Where's Harley?

KIRSTEN: Are you all right?

DAVIS: Kirsten Sabo, you can't be in here, why are you in here?

KIRSTEN: I saw you go in and then I heard someone being sick.

DAVIS: Fair enough.

KIRSTEN: Come on. I'll take you outside.

DAVIS: But you just got here.

KIRSTEN: Come on Davis. You need some fresh air.

(Continuous: Clinton crosses the parking lot outside the gym.)

CLINTON: Jule? Julie! Julie! Please! Julie!

(Continuous: Dan and Amanda sitting together on the steps outside the gym, drinking punch from Dixie cups. We can hear the trumpeter playing America.*)*

AMANDA: We never found out, did we? Did you ever see him, the person playing the trumpet?

DAN: Will you call me once in a while? I mean it's not like you're leaving town or anything.

AMANDA: Dan? Did you?

DAN: 'Cause I would like to call you.

AMANDA: Danny, I'm asking you!

DAN: Sure I've seen him. I met him, I know him. You all thought he was a student, right? Some pimply guy who all he did was practice day and night.

AMANDA: You know him?

DAN: All anybody had to do was go up there to the Music Annex and knock on the door.

AMANDA: Of course. Leave it to you. Oh, what the hell. *(Amanda kisses Dan—a good one.)*

DAN: I'll always love you.

AMANDA: So what's he like? He's not a student?

DAN: Wow. Okay. He's a kind of student. He's old. He's a Negro, Clinton was right. He's from Oklahoma.

AMANDA: Oh, god. Danny.

DAN: No, he is. And he has the power, with his trumpet, to tame all the fish in all the lakes and all the oceans, and to tame the wild beasts, and people, and everything there is, he has the power to tame it. And all he does, all day, all night, is practice. Till he gets it right.

AMANDA: *(finally)* I'll call you. I'll call you for sure.

(Kirsten enters parking lot, leading Davis.)

DAVIS: Oh, yeah. This is better. Where's Harley.

KIRSTEN: I knew it would be.

DAVIS: Oh, yeah. Oxygen, amazing. Why did I come? I didn't even have a date.

KIRSTEN: I don't have a date, and I'm here.

DAVIS: Loved the punch, I'm sure. You're really sweet, you know, Kirsten?

KIRSTEN: You don't need to keep saying that, okay Davis? It's starting to make me sick.

DAVIS: I gotta warn Harley. Harley? Harley!

KIRSTEN: You came with Harley?

DAVIS: That stuff in that bottle is some kind of poison. Harley! Don't drink whatever's in that bottle! Bourbon! Bourbon is poison! It's poison!

(Kirsten and Davis cross off; Melissa and Julie cross the parking lot.)

MELISSA: Hey. Come on, it's okay. It's gonna be okay.

JULIE: Oh, yeah. I know. I know.

MELISSA: He's just. You know. It's not easy.

JULIE: I know.

(Harley lurches on toward Amanda, carrying a package.)

HARLEY: This is for you.

AMANDA: Harley.

HARLEY: This is for you. From me. *(He gives Amanda the package.)*

DAN: Hey. Listen. You're a little drunk, you know?

HARLEY: It's for her, it's not for you.

DAN: Just take it easy, okay?

HARLEY: I wouldn't talk to me right now, Dan.

AMANDA: Harley, please. I'm sorry if I upset you.

HARLEY: If! Sorry, I'm sorry. Please. Open it. I want you to have it.
(Amanda opens the box.)

AMANDA: Oh, Harley. I can't take this.

HARLEY: Please.

AMANDA: Thank you. But I can't.

HARLEY: It's a movie camera! It's a Bell & Howell!

AMANDA: Take this back, Harley. Wherever you got it, just take it back.
(Clinton crosses on; from another direction Davis and Kirsten enter.)

CLINTON: *(converging)* Julie!

DAVIS: *(converging)* Harley!
(Melissa and Julie enter the parking lot.)

HARLEY: *(to Amanda)* What about. What about the hairs on the back of
my neck?

AMANDA: Harley, you're drunk.

HARLEY: What about my hands, he said you love my hands.

DAN: Harley, don't bother her, okay?
(Harley hits Dan hard in the face.)

DAVIS: Harley!

AMANDA: Get out! Get away!

CLINTON: Mandy?

JULIE: Clinton?

DAN: Fucker.

HARLEY: You said you were crazy about me, you told Davis you loved my
smile and my eyes and my hands!

AMANDA: I never. Said anything like that! Ever!

DAVIS: Harley.

CLINTON: Harley, get away from her.

HARLEY: You told him you loved my hands!

AMANDA: I hate your hands!

DAVIS: Harley, goddammit, leave her alone!
(Harley sees Davis.)

HARLEY: *(finally)* You made it up. That was you talking. Faggot. Faggot.
(Davis stands alone, all eyes on him.)

AMANDA: *(finally)* Oh, god, Davis.

HARLEY: There's your boyfriend, Mandy.

CLINTON: Okay, Harley. Just get out of here now.

HARLEY: *(to Amanda)* You two have a real good time.

CLINTON: Just leave her alone now, Harley, okay?

HARLEY: Keep the camera. Fuck you all.

CLINTON: It's all over.

JULIE: *(to Melissa)* Get somebody.

HARLEY: It sure as hell is.

(Melissa runs off.)

CLINTON: It's all over. Just get out of here now, okay?

HARLEY: You after another white woman, nigger?

CLINTON: Okay, man. *(Clinton moves on Harley.)*

DAVIS: Harley!

JULIE: Clinton!

KIRSTEN: Davis, don't!

(Davis comes between Harley and Clinton, tries to restrain Harley, and in a single motion Harley flings Davis off, whips a Barlow knife out, Clinton puts up his hands, one swipe, two swipes, it's over. Clinton looks at his hands. They're running with blood.)

HARLEY: Oh, god, I'm sorry. I'm sorry, I'm sorry, I'm sorry, I'm sorry, I'm sorry…

(Davis slowly gets up off the ground. The others stand, Julie tearing a handkerchief in two and wrapping Clinton's hands with them. The trumpeter softly plays Leaning On the Everlasting Arm.*)*

DAVIS: *(finally)* Clinton wasn't badly hurt. Just some blood and a lot of anger.

HARLEY: I'm sorry.

DAVIS: Harley was sent back to what used to be called "reform school" and then he dropped out of sight. I got through the senior year as the class homo, and then I made like Nathan Hale, went to New York and never came back. Once in a while, when I'm on the road, I check the phone book in my hotel room.

HARLEY: You might be an accident, but you're not a mistake.

DAVIS: I've found quite a few DeYoungs, but I've never called any of them. Amanda's still living in town.

AMANDA: I have dreams, dammit.

DAVIS: She married some other guy first, of course.

AMANDA: I have dreams.

DAVIS: But Dan, he doesn't give up.

DAN: I'm famous!

DAVIS: And I am telling you, their children are beautiful.

DAN: Famous!

DAVIS: Kirsten. I do remember you. I didn't think I did but I do.

KIRSTEN: You were the first boy who ever kissed me.

DAVIS: I remember.

(Melissa runs on.)

MELISSA: He wasn't even supposed to be there!

DAVIS: Melissa's a lawyer.

MELISSA: He was just crashing on the floor for a night!

DAVIS: Back in those days you could hitchhike and Clinton was going to check out schools, Columbia, Johns Hopkins. He hitched his way to Madison, then Cleveland, where he had the phone number of a friend of a friend.

MELISSA: The cops shot him! They bust in the door and they shot everybody, they shot all the Panthers and they shot Clinton dead!

DAVIS: There wasn't much press coverage, not like the big deal they made of the F.B.I. shoot-up in Chicago the year before. Our junior year. The year Clinton decided to become a doctor.

JULIE: Oh, god. He looks just like his mother dressed him up for church.

(Kirsten puts her arm around Julie.)

KIRSTEN: Bambi's mother died when he was young, and Bambi got through it, isn't that right?

DAVIS: Scarecrow?

CLINTON: Do not. Do that.

DAVIS: I think I miss you most of all.

KIRSTEN: After he got through all the troubles and the dangers that he found in the forest, Bambi had a good life, isn't that right?

JULIE: *(to Davis)* Whatever happened to *you?*

DAVIS: Right. Okay. I live in a suburb of New York, with Harold. I book travel things for tourists, wealthy ones. He's an account exec. He's a good guy, Harold. A little quiet. In a lot of ways he's great. But it's not what I pictured either. Okay, we done here?

CLINTON: The postcard?

DAVIS: Right. The postcard. It was addressed to me, care of my mother. Postmarked Phoenix. Mom called me in New York. It said…

HARLEY: "Remember our club?"

DAVIS: Words are never cheap, they almost always cost the earth.

HARLEY: "We had some good times, didn't we? Love, Harley."
DAVIS: Nathan Hale regretted he had but *one* life. Maybe he got off easy.
CLINTON: Maybe.
DAVIS: Right.
CLINTON: Go ahead.
DAVIS: You mean it?
CLINTON: I mean it.
DAVIS: *(to us)* Done!
　　(Lights out.)

END OF PLAY

EVERY SEVENTEEN MINUTES THE CROWD GOES CRAZY!

by Paul Zindel

BIOGRAPHY

Paul Zindel was awarded the 1971 Pulitzer Prize for his play *The Effect of Gamma Rays on Man-in-the-Moon Marigolds*. The play also garnered the Drama Critics Circle Award, an Obie, and several other awards that season. He is the author of several other plays, including *And Miss Reardon Drinks a Little, The Secret Affairs of Mildred Wild* and *Ladies at the Alamo,* all presented on Broadway, and *Amulets Against the Dragon Forces,* presented at the Circle Repertory Company. Mr. Zindel is the author of a dozen novels for young adults, including *The Pigman; Pardon Me, You're Stepping on my Eyeball,* and *I Never Loved Your Mind* (selected as one of *The New York Times'* Outstanding Books of the Year). His most recent novels are *The Amazing and Death-Defying Diary of Eugene Dingman* (1988), and *David and Della* (1993). He has also published a memoir *The Pigman and Me.* Mr. Zindel has written an adult novel, *When a Darkness Falls,* and several teleplays for PBS and the networks. *Let Me Hear You Whisper* was originally presented on television starring Ruth White; it was presented on *Arts and Entertainment* recently in a new production starring Jean Stapleton and Rue McClanahan. Other television productions include *Alice in Wonderland/Through the Looking-Glass,* and *Babes in Toyland.* Films include *Up the Sandbox, Runaway Train,* and *Maria's Lovers.*

AUTHOR'S NOTE

My play, *Every Seventeen Minutes the Crowd Goes Crazy!,* might never have come into existence if its director Craig Slaight had not awarded me a commission to write for the ACT's Young Conservatory in San Francisco. For the first time in many years, I was encouraged to let my muse lead me where it would—and I was terrified. The first hint of inspiration came to me six months before the play was scheduled to be performed. My own children had left to go to college. My wife had become absorbed in her career. I felt lonely and freaked out. It was not outlandish that a voice told me that the play I would write would be about kids whose parents had fled their family. That was to me the critical issue of the Nineties. Was the idea of "family" dying? Why were there so many reports of adults abdicating their roles as mothers and fathers? Why were more children left alone at home or allowed to prowl the streets at night?

I suspected that the play would have to be a sardonic comedy to explore its theme with any entertainment and balance. The muse next told me I needed a big cast. I wanted as many kids as possible on that stage, young actors with a chance to shine in the spotlight. Actors are such needful, magnificent humans. If they are true actors, they never really come alive unless they are on a stage. I knew that was my job as a playwright at the Young Conservatory. With my extraordinary director, we invented the Oprah-Speak Gap Chorus. The media had created a new literacy of madness that I wanted to capture in this tale of deserted young people. Magazines, TV, radio, and newspapers seemed primarily aimed at boggling the minds of adults and kids alike. Adult readers were snared by headlines and advertisements designed to let them know how inadequate they were. I would have the chorus ask the questions of the tabloids: *Why aren't you rich? Why don't you bungee jump? Why don't you grow Kombucha magic mushrooms?* And kids were inadequate if they didn't *buy Reeboks, shop like Tori Spelling, or own a butt-kicking portable gym.*

After the chorus, my muse led me to develop eight brothers and sisters who had been abandoned by their parents. They would be the central characters of the play. They were kids who were comic, daring, entrepreneurial, frightened, amazing, brave, and emotional. They were young people who, when all the surfaces were burnished and scraped clean, desperately wanted their parents to come home and for life to continue as they had known it once—a life where there were meals shared together, holidays, deep caring, and support.

Finally I met the young actors who would play the parts I was writing. The director and I got to know them well during the rehearsal period. For the first two weeks we explored the characters of my play. We used improvisations, interviews, and theater exercises to plumb the memories and dreams of the cast—for many of these young people were living the stuff of the comedy and anguish in my play. They gave of their hearts and souls to make the characters come alive. We were united on a great adventure to solve a disturbing human mystery. There in San Francisco that summer, we laughed and cried together. For a brief and glorious time we became a happy, loving family.

Paul Zindel

ORIGINAL PRODUCTION

Every Seventeen Minutes the Crowd Goes Crazy! was commissioned for and first presented through the New Plays Program at the Young Conservatory, American Conservatory Theater (Carey Perloff, Artistic Director), San Francisco, California. It was directed by Craig Slaight; lighting by Kelly Roberson; sound by Nathan Kish; costumes coordinated by Callie Floor, and the assistant director was Sara Whitaker. The cast was as follows:

Josh	Andrew Cohen
Gabby	Chelsea Peretti
Wendy	Tara Taylor
Stevie	Thomas Gorman
Jimmy	Milo Ventimiglia
Cora	Katie Giessler
J.P.	John Turnbull
Betsy	Carmen Molinari
John	Nicholas Hongola
Ann	Amanda Rowan
Ulie	Eli Marienthal
Maureen	Rebecca White
Dan	Kevin Crook
Dave	Adam Costello

The members of the ensemble also appeared in The Oprah-Speak Gap Chorus.

CHARACTERS

ULIE: young, 8 to 12—highly vulnerable, he breaks our hearts with his need, desperate to be loved, to feel secure; he cries himself to sleep everynight; his greatest pain is that the family is breaking up. He has lines around the epiphany of the play that go like this: "I WANT OUR FAMILY. WHY CAN'T WE KEEP OUR FAMILY AND NOT LET IT GO AWAY? DON'T LET IT GO AWAY! DON'T!"

DAVE: one of the older kids—sardonic, great sense of humor, attractive. We love him on first sight, and would like him to be our son, our friend.

MAUREEN: wants to be a magazine writer; she's gorgeous to watch because of her hair and that she is a thing in motion at all times. She's her brother Dave's age, give or take; she's lost in her own articulateness and she's terribly cunning with her beauty; she runs around the apartment houses making believe she's collecting for Catholic Charities whenever she needs money to treat her boyfriends for a date. She's hot as a pistol. She's a young Marilyn Monroe on speed and with a high IQ—tarot cards, other-world experiences, waiting to be abducted by aliens.

DAN: he's glad the family is gone. He'll take over. A fast food freak. He wants to be a politician or a lawyer.

OPRAH-SPEAK GAP CHORUS:

JOSH: wants to be a nose or an opera singer, own furniture and build a house where you can charge admission to it.

GABBY: a babbling actress.

STEVE: a computer freak—internet—a neo-hippie, freakish, disheveled shocker.

WENDY: shops, and goes to a school with spirit

JIMMY: a soccer player.

CORA: wants to be accepted into Brown University.

J.P.: wants to be a lawyer, conversant; articulate like his mother.

BETSY: a bowler.

JOHN: Bible and religious freak.

ANN: wants to be a vogue dancer.

TIME

Now, the end of our century.

SETTING

The living room and hallways of an American home. It is in chaos, as though a lot of kids have been living there for two months with no supervision—which is exactly the situation. Underneath the clutter of strewn clothes, old food containers, out-of-place furniture, and so forth. are remnants of a warm and gracious home.

EVERY SEVENTEEN MINUTES THE CROWD GOES CRAZY!

Mama Cass sings opening to "Dedicated to the One I Love" in the dark. The lights come up dim on living room. The Oprah-Speak Gap Chorus slowly assemble around the living room, ritualistically forming a circle, holding hands. Suddenly they turn out to audience as the music fades and the lights brighten.

CHORUS: *Were the parents naughty in the Time of Oprah-speak,*
Or was it the children who were naughty as can be?
Who was it that caused this great transfiguring
Or was it all a virtual reality?
(Chorus members step out and toward the audience with each of the following lines.)
JOSH: You could have been a basso profundo.
GABBY: Or given birth while bungee jumping.
WENDY: Or plucked your eyebrows bald!
STEVIE: In the game of life we use money to keep score.
JIMMY: Why aren't you a rock star?
CORA: A drunken mortician accidentally cremated a chihuahua.
J.P.: Do you own tax-free bonds?
BETSY: Three common kitchen spices could raise your IQ.

JOHN: Cure arthritis with a beer made by monks!

ANN: Amazing Mom lives with half a brain.

(Chorus moves randomly about the room, frequently crawling over the furniture.)

JOSH & GABBY: The two-headed baby is doing great!

STEVIE, WENDY & JIMMY: All things are possible except for skiing through a revolving door.

CORA & J.P.: Would you like to know twenty-five ways to train your husband?

(Chorus freezes.)

BETSY, JOHN & ANN: Stress is the overwhelming desire to beat the stuffing out of someone who deserves it!

(Chorus moves again.)

JOSH, GABBY & STEVIE: Some folks get high by licking toads.

WENDY, JIMMY & CORA: You really could have been Norman Schwarzkopf!

J.P., BETSY & JOHN: Are you rich and famous?

JOSH: Do you know a diplomat?

GABBY: All intellectual advances arise from leisure.

JIMMY: Women's Bodies…

WENDY: Women's Wisdom.

JIMMY, CORA, J.P. & BETSY: You could have broken into television.

(freeze)

JOHN, ANN, JOSH, GABBY & STEVIE: Paranoid schizophrenics outnumber their enemies two to one!

(moving again)

ANN: Grow Kombucha magic mushrooms!

JOHN: Be a producer!

BETSY: Direct!

J.P.: Be an A Plus Model.

ANN: *(repeating)* Amazing Mom lives with half a brain.

ALL: *(repeating)* The two-headed baby is doing great!

CORA: Did you give your child mental blocks for Christmas?

WENDY & STEVIE: What you say…

GABBY & JOSH: Is what you are!

JOSH: Sell on the phone.

JOSH & GABBY: Perform angelic healing.

JOSH, GABBY & STEVIE: Learn how to mambo.

JOSH, GABBY, STEVIE & WENDY: Cater, waltz, open a Starbuck's coffee bar.

ALL: Re-imagine the Divine!

ANN: Have a mega-memory.

ALL: Understand your cat.

ANN & JOHN: Meet the Mac.

ANN, JOHN & BETSY: Get the man.

ANN, JOHN, BETSY & J.P.: Marry rich.

ANN, JOHN, BETSY, J.P. & CORA: A pat on the back could have been a kick in the pants.

(Chorus breaks into a wild dance.)

ALL: *You just gotta sing!*

Have perfect abs and Swing

Enter the New Millennium and decide:

(Chorus freezes facing audience.)

Were the parents naughty in the Time of Oprah-speak,

Or was it the children who were naughty as can be?

Who was it that caused this great transfiguring

Or was it all a virtual reality?

(The Chorus quickly exits in all directions as Ulie comes into the living room. The lights come up bright, normal afternoon. He takes a garment bag out of a closet, climbs into it, and tries to zipper himself inside it. He doesn't get the zipper all the way up, but does a pretty good job, and starts to roll on the floor—we worry he's suffocating.

Maureen enters with suitcase, at first unaware of Ulie. She sets her suitcase down and begins to look for other family members. When she notices the moving garment bag, she at first freezes, frightened. Finally she approaches the bag.)

MAUREEN: Ulie? Is that you in there, Ulie?

ULIE: Yes. Yeah—it's me. *(Pops his head out—then quickly zips it back up.)*

MAUREEN: Why are you doing that? Why?

ULIE: What? Why am I doing what?

MAUREEN: You could hurt yourself—you really could.

ULIE: I didn't zipper it all the way up like little Stevie-Dillon-did.

MAUREEN: I don't care what little Stevie Dillon did. I care what *you* do.

ULIE: *(still rolling)* His mother had his father arrested.

MAUREEN: Stop that now!

ULIE: She really thought they both wanted to knock her off—and she started beating Stevie...

MAUREEN: *(goes to sofa)* Get out of that bag, Ulie!

ULIE: But he held her off with an egg beater—so she called the cops. And you think I'm kidding! *(Getting out of bag.)* Are you home for good?

MAUREEN: I don't know.

ULIE: Why don't you know?

MAUREEN: Dan called me…

ULIE: About what?

MAUREEN: About Peter and Jessica.

ULIE: What'd he say?

MAUREEN: Hey, don't you give your favorite sister a hug?

ULIE: *(goes to Maureen gives her a hug, joins her on the sofa)* I hope you didn't listen to him! Peter and Jessica came back. I was just talking to them.

MAUREEN: I wanted to make sure you were all right.

ULIE: They're in my room, Maureen—they came back last night. A little hung over. They had a nice time…

MAUREEN: Ulie, are you feeling okay today?

ULIE: Sure, I am.

MAUREEN: I spoke to Dave.

ULIE: Is he coming down?

MAUREEN: He said he was. I rang him in Bolton Landing. He's working at The House of Scotts.

ULIE: Did Dan call him, too? He had Stevie and J.P. searching the house, sucking up everything they could find.

MAUREEN: Dan called everyone. He wants us all here for a meeting—are you all right, Ulie?

ULIE: Yeah, I'm fine. *(gets up, returns bag to closet)* Stevie was looking for credit cards…J.P. was after the legal stuff.

MAUREEN: *(follows Ulie)* Look, honey, you know I love you…

ULIE: Sure I know it. Thanks.

MAUREEN: *(kneels to Ulie)* No matter what happens, I'll always be there for you, you know that, don't you?

ULIE: You don't have to worry about anything.

(Maureen turns away.)

ULIE: What's the matter.

MAUREEN: *(moves away)* I didn't say I was worried.

ULIE: *(pursuing)* Are you still hearing that thing in your head? That thing?

MAUREEN: Let's not talk about that…*(looks away.)*

ULIE: *(confronts her)* I want to know if you're still hearing it. You're still hearing it, aren't you?

MAUREEN: Yes—I'm hearing it. *(trying to change subject)* Vinny's picking me up later for a movie. *(getting a small collection container out of suitcase)* He has me collecting for Catholic Charities now. He likes going out a lot.

ULIE: Catholic Charities is paying for your dates?

MAUREEN: He wanted to make a seven o'clock show, but I told him I needed more time to get from house to house around here. There are more Catholics around his house.

ULIE: The kids at school think he's a member of The Black Hand—organized crime or something.

MAUREEN: I think it's because he has too much hair. He's very hairy.

ULIE: Does he still have his dream of one day owning a singles bar in the meat-packing section of town?

MAUREEN: He's nice to me, but I suppose it's better that Peter and Jessica…

ULIE: *(stomps away from Maureen)* They're in my room—I told you they're back.

MAUREEN: Come over here, Sunshine.

ULIE: *(hesitates, his back to Maureen. Finally, he joins her on sofa)* What's the Thing been saying to you? The Voice?

MAUREEN: I don't think we should talk about it, Ulie…

ULIE: It's something horrible, isn't it?

MAUREEN: I didn't say that.

ULIE: But I know it is.

MAUREEN: It comes after me now, Ulie…but I don't want you having any bad dreams.

ULIE: Is it here now? Is the Voice talking to you?

MAUREEN: Not right this second—I mean, I try not to think about it. It had gotten so bad, I stopped going outside for a while.

ULIE: Does it come when you're with Vinny?

MAUREEN: Vinny hears me, I mean, he knows it's freaking me out. It came into my head in a subway station.

ULIE: It wanted you to jump in front of a train, didn't it?

MAUREEN: It tried to choke me…I was eating a muffin and the Voice started to make my throat close.

ULIE: You've got to at least tell Mom.

MAUREEN: I've found a way to calm it. I know this is going to sound crazy…*(she starts rummaging through her suitcase)*…you're going to think I've really gone off the deep end. *(she takes out a large bag of taco chips) This* seems to keep it away…

ULIE: A bag of taco chips?

MAUREEN: I know it looks ridiculous...

ULIE: Taco chips?

MAUREEN: I don't think it's the taco chips, exactly—it's the crinkling of the bag.

ULIE: The sound of the crinkling shuts off the Voice?

MAUREEN: I know how loony tunes it sounds—I was on a roller coaster ride...

ULIE: It wanted you to jump?

MAUREEN: I kept trying to smile, pretend I was having a good time— while it was telling me to jump.

ULIE: Did it tell you to hold your hands up in the air?

MAUREEN: It wanted me to slip out from the safety rail—I was with Vinny, and the Thing was screaming in my ear...

ULIE: It told you to throw yourself out?

MAUREEN: I was shaking, and I was holding this bag of taco chips...I had the bag against my head, against my ear...

ULIE: And the voice stopped?

MAUREEN: Yes, it stopped. It sounded like an old man choking to death. You can't tell anyone about this, okay. It's got to be our secret or they'll put me away again. You understand that, don't you, Ulie?

ULIE: Oh yeah, I got that.

(Gabby and Wendy let themselves in. They're home from summer school lugging their back packs.)

GABBY: Hi, Ulie—Oh, hi, Maureen.

MAUREEN: Hi, Gabby.

WENDY: We were wondering if you were going to show up. Hi, Ulie.

ULIE: *(not thrilled with their interruption)* I'll be up in my room. *(He exits.)*

MAUREEN: *(gives Gabby and Wendy a reprimanding glare)* You weren't home over the weekend.

GABBY: *(handing Wendy her backpack, who puts both in closet)* How would you know?

MAUREEN: I called.

GABBY: *(sits)* We went to Olivia Schecter's Bat Mitzvah in Elmsford, but Dan called up with the news.

WENDY: *(hovers above Gabby's chair)* Warner Corbin, with the hare lip, was going to rent a stretch limo...

GABBY: We all ended up in a Winebago...

WENDY: Nobody had to worry about a driver peering through a limo partition at us making out.

MAUREEN: *(sits)* I don't think you should have left Ulie alone.

GABBY: Don't make it sound like we deserted him. He likes to be left alone.

WENDY: We check in.

GABBY: How do you think he's taking the news?

MAUREEN: He says Peter and Jessica are in his room.

GABBY: I wish you'd stop referring to Mom and Dad as Peter and Jessica.

WENDY: *(kneeling at coffee table, starting to take fishing sinkers out of her hair)* It ticks me off, too.

MAUREEN: Wendy, are those fishing sinkers?

WENDY: Yeah.

MAUREEN: You're wearing fishing sinkers in your hair?

WENDY: Yeah, they make me weigh more. Olivia Schecter's mother is the school nurse...

GABBY: She catches Wendy trying to throw up all the time.

WENDY: She caught me with my finger down my throat in the lunch room last month.

MAUREEN: Wendy, if you have a problem...

GABBY: She says Wendy's bulimic anorexic.

WENDY: She weighs me whenever she sees me. Weighed me at a mall once.

GABBY: *(picks up Maureen's bag of taco chips, opens and starts to eat)* She says if Wendy loses any more weight she's going to have to talk to the Department of Health...

WENDY: Or our parents...

GABBY: And we don't want that, now do we?

MAUREEN: I'm worried about you, Wendy...

(Gabby and Wendy exchange a look.)

WENDY: Well, we're worried about you.

GABBY: Yeah.

MAUREEN: Was it another fax?

WENDY: That's all they ever send.

GABBY: They can't even stand talking to us.

MAUREEN: Where from?

GABBY: Some trotting race track in Ohio. Northfield Park—They said it's beautiful. No racing December 24.

WENDY: They said it's really a great place and that every nineteen minutes the place goes crazy.

GABBY: But they're leaving there. They heard there's a track in Virginia where the races are run within seventeen minutes.

WENDY: So like, every seventeen minutes now the crowd can go crazy.

GABBY: Yeah...

WENDY: And they heard somebody in California is building a new double track...

GABBY: Double stable, double starting gates, double wagering...

WENDY: So every *nine* minutes the place can go crazy.

GABBY: They can't wait until that track opens.

WENDY: Last week they were at trotters in Chicago.

GABBY: That was the week before—last week was St. Louis.

WENDY: They said when they're not at the trotters they're at a Native American casino.

GABBY: They look for new ones where most of the blackjack dealers don't quite know what they're doing yet.

WENDY: They're winning enough so they don't need to work anymore!
(All three become silent.)

GABBY: Did you know I've been seeing this guy *Max?*

MAUREEN: No.

GABBY: He's nice but a little strange in that he likes his parents.

WENDY: He's the son of a late marriage...

GABBY: It just happened that these old people gave birth to him...

MAUREEN: Are you in love with him?

WENDY: He's been asking her where Peter and Jessica are.

GABBY: Now you've got her doing it.

WENDY: What's she going to tell him?

GABBY: On a scale of one to ten I love him a three. *You can't meet my parents because they've run away from home and they're never coming back!*

WENDY: *They're just going to spend the rest of their lives going from one trotting race track and Native American casino to the next...*

GABBY: *For ever and ever...*

WENDY: *And they never want to see us again!*

MAUREEN: They said that?

GABBY: Read my lips— *"Never coming back!"*

WENDY: That's what they faxed us this time.

GABBY: It flipped me into a food binge at the Bat Mitzvah!

WENDY: *(getting up to get water bottle from her backpack)* You were disgusting.

GABBY: *(snapping to Wendy)* I know that. *(To Maureen)* We got there and I knew I was emotionally vulnerable.

MAUREEN: Gabby, you know you have trouble with food.

WENDY: She asked if she could help put out the food platters.

GABBY: *(in defense to Wendy)* I started with an Overeater's Anonymous abstinent meal.

WENDY: Pasta, tossed salad, sliced beef and a slice of whole wheat bread.

GABBY: Like I was really in control...

WENDY: But she started to graze.

GABBY: I mixed with the normal kids and ate shrimp, egg rolls, baked ziti, designer pizza, baby quiches, salmon, whitefish, creamed herring, and humus dip.

WENDY: It was a great dip with just a touch of jalapenos.

MAUREEN: I don't need to know everything you ate!

GABBY: *(moves to sit next to Maureen)* Then I felt mentally strange.

MAUREEN: Mentally strange?

GABBY: *(patting Maureen's shoulder)* I mean, by *our* standards.

WENDY: She disappeared. I couldn't find her.

GABBY: *(defying Maureen)* I started fixing plates of baguettes, sliced Brie, curried buffalo wings, moussaka, crab cakes, hot sausages, deviled eggs, caviar, linguini, and Clams Casino.

WENDY: This was like the *start.*

GABBY: *(begins enacting the event)* I was shoving the food into my mouth, hiding behind the band.

WENDY: Cute drummer. You were such a pig.

MAUREEN: Don't call your sister that.

WENDY: *(rises, challenging)* Don't tell me what I can say and can't say.

GABBY: *(demanding attention)* I waited until the games and free party Polaroid shot sessions...

WENDY: The ones framed with balloons. They also had *Make Your Own T-Shirt,* karaoke, and Vogue dancers dressed like giant lobsters on stilts...

GABBY: Everyone else was away from the desserts...

WENDY: She laced into the cake.

GABBY: You didn't see me.

WENDY: You told me what you did.

GABBY: I started eating straight from the trays, pushing ladyfingers, strudels, chocolate-covered strawberries, cheese cake, vanilla mousse…

MAUREEN: That's sick.

WENDY: Petit fours, wildberry tarts, creme caramel, and a *Make Your Own Ice Cream Sundae* bar!

GABBY: My heart was pounding!

WENDY: She took a tray of food outside and hid on a dark terrace.

GABBY: *(on her knees behind coffee table)* I went into a food trance. I had a large loaf of French bread, and I was smearing desserts onto the bread…

WENDY: Everything in the dark started to taste like sand.

GABBY: I'd been eating for over five hours…

WENDY: *(hands over her ears)* I have to cover my ears or I'll engage in reverse peristalsis!

GABBY: I was pressing the food into my mouth.

WENDY: She didn't know what anything was anymore…

GABBY: Grace Applebaum and her date…

WENDY: Last year's valedictorian…

GABBY: Came out onto the terrace…

WENDY: They almost caught her…

GABBY: I went back inside to the kitchen…

WENDY: I could upchuck right now.

GABBY: I looked down at the food tray in my hands. In the light I saw large red ants were crawling all over it—and I felt specks crawling around my lips…

WENDY: Ants!

GABBY: Bugs all over the food I was chewing…

MAUREEN: How disgusting.

WENDY: I told you. And she didn't spit anything out…

GABBY: I was so ashamed but then I did something so terrible, so *destructive*…

WENDY: She started poking the rest of the food on the tray…

GABBY: Looking for pieces of food the ants weren't on.

WENDY: She was out of her mind!

GABBY: I started to cry—and Mrs. Schecter came up to me and said, "Oh, Gabby, aren't you going to dance? Aren't you going to dance?" *(she bursts into tears)*

MAUREEN: *(going to her, but Gabby pushes her away)* Oh, Gabby. *(Finally she offers Gabby some taco chips, which she accepts.)*

WENDY: *(after watching them a moment)* So if Mom isn't coming home anymore, then I guess her clothes are all ours. *(She opens the closet and starts pulling out her mother's coats.)* I always wanted a fun fur! *(Gabby breaks from Maureen, climbing over coffee table, joins Wendy and starts grabbing some clothes herself.)*

GABBY: Hey, you pick one—I pick one!
(Their grabbing escalates and they start pushing and shoving each other around the room.)

MAUREEN: *(trying to break up the fight)* Can't you wait? Can't you wait until our meeting? Wait! Stop it! Stop!
(Dan barges in with two pals, Josh and Jimmy. They're lugging big speakers and boxes of party food, and so on.)

DAN: *(a jolly despot to his buddies)* Set the speakers up! Gotta get the drinks and ice into the refrigerator. Blow up balloons. *(Seeing Maureen trying to break up Gabby and Wendy)* Hey, sisters—don't tear those threads!

GABBY: Get Maureen off our backs!

WENDY: Yeah.

MAUREEN: They're taking Mom's clothes!

DAN: What do they say about an ill wind!

JIMMY: Hi, Maureen, Gabby!

JOSH: *(a real crush)* Hey, Wendy.

GABBY: What's going on, Danny?

WENDY: What's with the speakers?

JIMMY: *(an arm around Wendy and Gabby)* If you girls are gonna rumble, we can throw in mud fights and charge for them, too.

DAN: We're starting parties!

WENDY: You're having a party tonight?

JOSH: *(trying to get Wendy's attention)* I saw you at Olivia's Bat Mitzvah. *(Dan motions Josh to take boxes into kitchen, which Josh reluctantly does.)*

MAUREEN: *(to Dan)* You said you were calling a meeting.

DAN: Meeting first, then a party. *(To girls)* This'll be the dance floor.

JOSH: *(returning)* Your parents really aren't coming back?

MAUREEN: Hey, it's all right for us to talk about it, not you.

JIMMY: *(sits next to Wendy)* Hey, Wendy. I got the part of Dracula in the summer school musical. Mr. Schaffer liked the way my eyes went like *this!*

WENDY: Nice.

JIMMY: I wish my parents would disappear for good, too.

DAN: *(to Maureen)* I heard Vinny borrowed you a rental car last week and you left it on a sidewalk.

MAUREEN: He was kidding. What's the meeting about?

GABBY: Let's have it now.

WENDY: Maureen said Dave's coming down.

MAUREEN: We've got to wait for him.

DAN: *(takes clipboard out of his pack and puts pack in closet)* No, we don't. We don't have to wait for anyone anywhere.

GABBY: They let you come down from Scout camp?

JOSH: They were glad to get rid of him.

DAN: I quit.

WENDY: Peggy Argenziano's brother said you were in charge of the waterfront activities.

DAN: Yeah, it was great.

JOSH: You should have seen him fish for sunnies.

JIMMY: He used Fruity Pebbles cereal for bait—just threw it on the water.

JOSH: When the sunnies came to the top, he'd sock 'em with a hammer!

DAN: Hey, that's not true. You're scaring my sisters.

MAUREEN: I've got to collect for Catholic Charities a while—I'll be back. Vinny's supposed to pick me up.

DAN: Too bad. I was hoping you'd handle the tickets.

GABBY: What tickets?

WENDY: What's going on?

DAN: We've got to get something going.

JIMMY: You ought to open up one of those bagel places, like Cy Friedman did last year.

JOSH: He makes a couple a hundred thousand a year from coffee and bagels—didn't even bother going to college.

GABBY: I like his blueberry ones, scooped, with low-fat cream cheese.

WENDY: He like invented the scooped bagel.

DAN: Kids got nowhere to go—that's where we come in.

JIMMY: I know a kid in Tenafly who runs a party house—his parents took off just like yours.

MAUREEN: You don't talk about our parents.

JOSH: They charge ten, twenty dollars a night just for admission an a couple of drinks.

JIMMY: He uses a sliding fee...He sends out announcements...

JOSH: To everyone in the yearbook...

JIMMY: Especially the losers.

JOSH: The kids who like never made it socially...

JIMMY: Yeah.

JOSH: They think they're getting an invitation...

JIMMY: You make it look and sound like they're special and they're good enough to be invited to a party—and that they're going to meet lots of friends...

DAN: I was thinking we could call the place The Cheetah!

GABBY: I like it.

WENDY: Yeah, jungle is good.

JIMMY: You babes can stick around, dance with some of the losers a while.

DAN: Help make them have a good time.

JOSH: *(to Wendy)* I want a dance, too.

DAN: It's gonna work.

GABBY: *(to Wendy)* Let's check the closets in their bedroom. I want that silver sequined thing she got.

WENDY: I get some of the DKNY stuff.

GABBY: I wonder if she took the Beneton, the sweat shirt I liked with Einstein on it.

(The girls start off toward the master bedroom. Suddenly Ulie comes charging at them with two mannequins in a wheelchair that are dressed as Peter and Jessica. The girls scream at the bizarre sight.)

ULIE: You keep out of their room! You keep out!

GABBY: Are you nuts?

WENDY: Get out of our way!

ULIE: Dan, I caught Stevie and J.P. sucking up the plastic and pin numbers.

MAUREEN: Leave him alone.

DAN: Hey, Ulie babe, how're you doin'?

GABBY: *(to Ulie)* Get out of my way!

ULIE: *(to the girls)* Get away! *(To Dan)* You told them to slurp up everything and head for the bank.

WENDY: *(to Dan)* Will you get rid of him?

GABBY: *(focusing on the Mom mannequin dress)* I want that dress.

ULIE: Get your hands off it! Dan, call off the creeps.

JOSH: *(sees sweater on Dad mannequin)* If no one wants the sweater, I'd take it.

ULIE: *(pushes wheelchair at Josh causing him to stumble and fall)* Get away, you bloodsucker!

DAN: *(gets up)* Hey, come on, Ulie...

GABBY: Get those dummies out of Grandma's wheelchair.

WENDY: You're really freaking me out!

(Ulie uses the wheelchair as a shield to block his brothers and sisters as they close in on him.)

ULIE: *(crying out pathetically)* They're coming back! I'm telling about the plastic.

(Dave enters.)

DAVE: He's right!

(The others turn and see Dave as he comes into the room. His appearance is a clear threat to Dan's rule.)

DAN: Hi, Dave.

DAVE: Dan—hello.

GABBY: What're you talking about, "he's right?"

DAVE: Pete and Jessica are coming back. I saw them.

ULIE: I told you freak-a-rino!

MAUREEN: You saw them?

WENDY: How could you see them?

GABBY: You were at Lake George!

DAVE: I took a bus to Northfield Park.

MAUREEN: You found them in the mob at the trotters?

DAVE: Mom always stands at the finish line. *(Dave crosses to Ulie and gives him a hug.)* You having a party, Dan?

ULIE: I told you, mega freak-a-rino!

DAN: *(nailing Dave)* They said that?

MAUREEN: They said they're coming back?

DAVE: They're thinking about it.

GABBY: We got a fax.

DAVE: Hey, I talked to them.

DAN: When they comin'?

DAVE: They wanted a day to think about it.

ULIE: When are they coming, Dave?

DAVE: They said they'd call us tonight.

DAN: They're not going to call.

GABBY: They fax!

WENDY: They're going to fax!

DAVE: They said they'd call, they said they're probably coming back.

DAN: They told you that to get rid of you. They probably dropped a brick when they saw you.

DAVE: *(to the others)* I need to talk to Dan.

JOSH: Hey, what about the party.

DAVE: There's not going to be a party.

JIMMY: Hey, Dan, is this a big wank or what?

DAN: You guys blow up the balloons, get the refreshments ready in the kitchen.

(They exit to kitchen.)

MAUREEN: *(Heading for the door with her Catholic Charities container and bag of taco chips. She puts them in her sack pocketbook.)* I got some collecting to do. I'll be back, Dave, okay?

DAVE: Take Ulie with you.

ULIE: No way—they'll sell off the furniture.

DAN: It's okay.

MAUREEN: Come on.

ULIE: I'm staying—they'd rip off Mom's clothes.

GABBY: We weren't ripping off anything.

WENDY: She's not coming back.

DAVE: They said they'd call around eight.

MAUREEN: I'm going, Ulie.

ULIE: Be careful.

(Maureen exits.)

GABBY: We're just checking Mom's closet.

WENDY: We'll divvy them up—the clothes—like in case...

GABBY: Yeah, like in case.

(They skirt Ulie who's still commandeering the mannequins. Wendy can't resist coping a scarf from the Mom mannequin as they exit— Blackout.)

(Spot on Gabby.)

GABBY: I noticed something was unusual when I found my father reading a law book and giggling during the chapter on child abandonment. When he started reading several books on Greek and Roman mythology, I should have known for certain he was going to clear out. He highlighted all the parts around the Fates and the Sybil, how children who were dangerous needed to be left in the hills. Oedipus. Romulus and Remus. Moses. Children whose heels were cut so wild animals could better stalk them. *(She shudders.)*

(Spot on Dan.)

DAN: The only thing I noticed different about my mother was the way she would sit around the house crying a lot—which, I suppose, is unusual for a psychotherapist. She seemed obsessed with the case history of this one child patient she had. She kept printing out copies of it and leaving it around our breakfast table and at the neighborhood ashrams and supermarkets. It was something horrible that had happened to a ten-year-old boy at Christmas. His parents were loaded. Filthy rich. The father was a Hollywood producer. His mother was a Mutual Funds feminist. And they wanted to surprise their son with the greatest Christmas ever—so they bought him wonderful things: a Schwinn 10-speed, rollerblades, a Lionel electric train set, skis, a sled, a tennis racket, a dog, candy, a BB pistol, a Swiss army knife—a Christmas tree flooded with gift-wrapped boxes and bows and tinsel everywhere. A huge living room crammed with presents and candy canes. They had created this dream for their son, and on Christmas morning, their son came down the stairs into the living room—this ten-year-old boy saw this fantasy they bought him—and he burst into tears! "What's the matter, son?" his father cried out, rushing to him, holding him, hugging him—"Is there something you had your heart set on that you don't see? Is there something we forgot?" And the kid, wailing through his tears said, "I don't know, but there *could* be. There *could* be!" And that was when his father pulled back his hand and slapped his son with all his might. He slapped him and slapped him and slapped him! *(Spot fades out on Dan. Lights come up as we hear the marching steps of the Oprah-speak Gap Chorus who take the stage chanting. Dan and Dave freeze. Ulie is part of the Chorus.)*

CHORUS: *Glamour, Beauty, A lifetime of fabulous skin,*
Wind Song, Reebok, Prince Matchabelli,
Bon Jovi, White Zombie, Crash Test Dummies,
Make great things happen with Jordache!
(Freezing in various glamorous poses, then sitting and standing all over the set.)

BETSY: *You did that on purpose!*

CORA: *Go to your room!*

BETSY: *Eat your brussel sprouts, zip your lip!*

ALL: *You think you're different than anyone else around here?*

ANN: You don't realize that when Tori Spelling gets a dress for a big bash, she also buys out every one like it in the store so no other star can show up in the same thing!

BETSY: I'll treat you like an adult when you start acting like one.

JIMMY: If a girl tells me I look familiar, I know she just wants to meet me. That's why for the close-up I need a butt-kicking portable gym. I want to look fresh now that guy virgins are in. I want to be on the cutting edge with the rest of the sweatfast hunks who push their limits in windsurfing, jetskiing, and hang-gliding—which is hard to do on the allowance you give me.

ALL: We're not made of money, you know.

J.P.: I only asked if we couldn't have a little Perrier around the house. Demi Moore spends three thousand dollars a month for her designer water, so I don't think a couple of lousy bottles of Perrier is asking too much.

CORA: Well, as long as you live in my house, you're going to behave like a decent human being.

BETSY: I think it's my duty to be a mega-babe, wear way-hot tiny tees, shape up a superbod for summer, participate in the string bikini fashion bonanza—and wear the new moisture whip lipstick from Maybeline.

STEVIE: I want to get toned on a sailboat.

JOSH: I need a weekend in Aspen.

ALL: How can you stand to live like this?

CORA: Johnny Depp has his walls covered with clowns and trashes hotel rooms.

BETSY: You're going to sit on that potty until I get some results!

WENDY: Drew Barrymore's very next tattoo is going to be a daisy! She says she dreams of having a field of daisies where she can take off all her clothes and go running through them!

JIMMY: Luke Perry has this recurring dream that he's going to die on his thirty-sixth birthday in a green Corvette.

ALL: We'll try no TV for a week and see if that brings you to your senses.

ULIE: David Copperfield made a munchkin appear for super model Claudia Schiffer.

CORA: It's your turn to wash the dishes.

GABBY: Madonna has a fleet of limos on 24-hour standby, a private jet, and eight boy toys.

BETSY: I don't personally see anything wrong with being a hedonist—decent food, shelter, warmth, and pleasure. I want to feel good at something, play with someone wearing the same uniform—basically I want to have a good time—and I think—if it feels good, I'm just going to do it.

ALL: And just where do you think you're going, young man?

ULIE: I'm just having a bad hair day. I'm going to need money for a perm, ultra-babe layers, or a bob that's cut just below the ear. Whatever I pick, I want it to be hot and in vogue!

BETSY & CORA: Urgent! Important! Attention!

ALL: New! Special! Just for you! *(beginning marching step again)*
Glamour, Beauty, A lifetime of fabulous skin,
Wind Song, Reebok, Prince Matchabelli,
Bon Jovi, White Zombie, Crash Test Dummies,
Make great things happen with Jordache!
(Freezes in pose, then exits quickly in every direction as Ulie swings the mannequins back into the action of Dan and Dave.)

DAN: You know Pete and Jessica aren't coming back.

ULIE: *(playing a game talking as dummies)* Yes, we are.

DAVE: *(checking his watch)* They'll call in twenty, thirty minutes.

DAN: They'll fax before the daily double.

ULIE: Hey, we said we're gonna call—we're gonna call!

DAN: *(to Ulie)* Cut it out, Ulie. *(yelling, rises, crosses toward kitchen)* The party's still on!

DAVE: Put it off, Dan.

ULIE: Yeah, Danny-Sonny boy.

DAN: I heard you're making forty to fifty bucks a night at the House of Scotts.
(Stevie and J.P. enter with papers, legal folders, and so on.)

STEVIE: Hey, Dave—you made it down.

DAVE: Hi, Stevie, J.P....

J.P.: *(moves toward wheelchair. Ulie pushes him away)* What's with the dummies.

ULIE: Don't call them dummies.

STEVIE: What? You got them dressed like Mom and Dad?

ULIE: No, they're Winona Ryder and the Jerky Boys.

DAN: What'd you find out?
(Ulie keeps shifting the wheelchair so the dummies continue to appear to be following the action. Dan sits, Stevie and J.P. report from either side of him.)

STEVIE: They had sixty-three cards—not the Guinness Book of Records, but close.

J.P.: I got the mortgage papers, stock certificates—a lot of legal stuff.

ULIE: *(using Mom's voice)* Bottom line it for 'em, boys.

STEVIE: I was at the ATM at Foodtown for three hours. Most of the plastic was maxed out.

J.P.: Most of the cards were in Dad's name—we found the second cards for Mom—most of the pin numbers were our birthdays.

ULIE: We were sentimental devils, weren't we!

DAN: What cash can we get?

STEVIE: Nothing on the sixty-two of them, but we found a Harris Bank card they must have forgotten.

J.P.: It was down behind the bed—it's got five thousand on it—all for cash advances.

STEVIE: We took out a thousand—the max for today—tomorrow we can get another thousand.

DAVE: Hey, it's not our money.

ULIE: Yeah! *(Shoves Stevie and J.P.)* I'm telling Maureen on you crooks! Then I'm going to squeal on her to the Pope! *(Ulie runs out.)*

DAVE: *(trying to stop Ulie…but it's too late)* Hey, it's getting dark!

DAN: What about stocks and bonds?

J.P.: Zip. They bought 50 shares of Hardman Axle on the day the president of the company died.

STEVIE: They got a second mortgage from a retarded bank in Louisiana and a third from the Money Store with lots of letters from Jim Palmer and Phil Rizzuto.

J.P.: The good news is I called a mess of the 800 numbers for the maxed plastic and they said they'll give higher lines of credit if we pay last month's interest.

DAVE: Dad had a good job.

DAN: You've been in the boondocks too long, Dave. They cut him to twenty hours a week—made him part-time status—no health plan, no pension…

STEVIE: We found the papers for that. The company left like only five percent full-timers.

J.P.: They paid the local gun shop to stay closed while the demotion and firing-notices were given out—to keep down the employee-related murder rate.

DAVE: Mom was working.

DAN: Hey, don't blame her. Mom's only mistake was that when it came to treating her patients, she was honest.

STEVIE: There were so many lunatics coming over here all the time.

DAN: She'd like have one or two sessions with them for fifty dollars a gig, then they'd realize she was nuttier than they were—send them to a psycho-pharmacologist—who'd put them on Prozac—they'd get such a buzz, she'd never see them again.

(Stevie and J.P. laugh—Dave turns away.)

DAN: Stevie—J.P., help the guys in the kitchen, okay?

(Stevie and J.P. head out leaving Dan and Dave—and the mannequins.)

DAVE: Talk to them when they call—tell them to come back.

DAN: Hey, don't be ticked off at them.

DAVE: Just talk to them.

DAN: They gave up. You can't blame them.

DAVE: They've got to come back...

DAN: Why?

DAVE: For Ulie...

DAN: Lighten up.

DAVE: We won't have a place...

DAN: You're making enough for an apartment.

DAVE: I'm renting a room...

DAN: We all can. I'll take care of Ulie.

DAVE: You don't understand...

DAN: What?

DAVE: The house where I'm staying...

DAN: What about it?

DAVE: It's this woman's—

DAN: So what?

DAVE: This family's.

DAN: Are there any babes?

DAVE: One—she's got a boyfriend. They've got a dog—a springer spaniel.

DAN: You know it's B.Y.O.B. for the first few parties—then we can move into kegs.

DAVE: Her name's Mrs. Cavucci, that's the family's name...

DAN: Even with Cokes, two bucks a can—we'll make money...

DAVE: They include me in on things. Like everybody wakes up, we eat breakfast together—then someone says "Hey, let's go on a picnic"—

and they grab their stuff and drive to a park. Play ball, sit on blankets, read books...

DAN: Sounds sappy.

DAVE: Yeah, it is—a lot of it. They're vegetarians—Mrs. Cavucci makes cauliflower cheese pie, and this other thing we call cheese flops. Cheese flops sucks...

DAN: It sounds like it...

DAVE: They're liberal, the parents—but they put the kids first, they're holding double jobs to put them through college. The father pays the car insurance for his son, an old VW bug—it goes *Vroom Vroom*...

DAN: I hate VW's...

DAVE: Yeah...

(A spot begins to isolate Dave as he drifts into a seemingly unsentimental, but poignant, dream of what a family can be.)

DAVE: At dinner they do this lame thing, we sit around the table and everyone tells one good thing that happened to them that day, and one rotten thing—and when you tell the bad thing, somebody says, "Hey, maybe I can help fix that." I don't mind hanging out there. It's sixty dollars a week. The room sucks. They've got photos all over the place. If one of the kids writes a poem, *Bam,* it gets glued up. And Mrs. Cavucci has this nun sitting on the fireplace mantle, it's really freaky, this foot tall carved nun that's holding a real inch size bible—they're not religious but they do Christmas and Hanukkah—they're like really crazy liberals. Stupid momentos all over the place...A really dumb Model T Ford sculpture that's mounted on a teaspoon. I mean a lot of crap. Mexican paintings. A candle snuffer. They've got junk we've never even thought of—but sometimes they all go out and I go upstairs—this white rug goes upstairs where their bedrooms are—quilts and worn Indian rugs all over the place, and writing desks and books...And I get dizzy. Sometimes I have to hold onto the railing, because it seems the whole house is flying through space—like it's some kind of big time capsule—a whole house hurtling through the universe—and it makes me feel I want to go with it...

(During the monologue, Gabby and Wendy have come out, silhouettes in party clothes of their mother's. J.P., Jimmy, Stevie, and Josh have also joined the tableau—bearing party balloons, snacks, and so forth. The lights come up on all and the scene springs into action.)

GABBY: *(about her sequined top/dress)* What do you think of this? It used to make Mom look cheap.

WENDY: This was Mom's favorite karaoke outfit. It's like so cheap it's happening.

J.P.: Where'd you want the chips and nuts? I found some stale Pringles.

DAN: *(pointing to coffee table)* Just put them down here. How can you find stale Pringles? *(To Jimmy)* Is the bar ready?

GABBY: Where are the paying guests? *(picking up bowl of chips)* What else you got to eat? What've we got left, Ragu Pizza Sauce and four cans of minestrone?

DAN: Who do we know who's definitely coming? Who paid twenty bucks? Like who do you know for sure?

JIMMY: I gave a load out in gym and homeroom—and at the auditions. You know, invitations.

JOSH: I gave them to every dork I saw. Civics class is like dork city.

STEVIE: We're going to end up with forty, fifty easy. I gave one to Catherine Zubecki, that sophomore with the plate in her head.

WENDY: Is this going to be nothing but losers? We're going to hostess losers?

GABBY: *(gets up)* I got dressed up for what? They're all going to look like stunt puppets from *The Dark Crystal!*

WENDY: I'm going to the bathroom.

GABBY: *(glaring at Dan)* Yeah, I'll stick my finger down my throat with you.

(Blackout—quick spot up on Cora dribbling a basketball—in a flash-back sequence to school that afternoon. Josh comes out of the shadows holding an invitation.)

JOSH: Hey, Cora!

CORA: Hi, Josh!

JOSH: You're getting really good at sinking hoops. I was wondering what you were doing this weekend, like tonight?

CORA: *(tosses him the ball, hard)* Cutting a stencil for the Student Advocate Group. Did you see the flyers we gave out proving bicycle riding is a hazard to male fertility?

JOSH: They were cool.

(Tosses ball back. Cora shoots. Josh takes rebound. Cora goes to Josh to take ball. Josh hangs on—so they both hold ball.)

CORA: The big news is Louie Pincheck, my co-president, and Janet

Moravian, we're going international. We want to stop goat-tossing in Spain and dwarf-tossing in Munich.

JOSH: Hey, I read about that in the paper. You've got guts, the way you protest.

CORA: We're going to be bigger than Greenpeace, doing an Internet and mailgram blitz on Madrid. Germany only throws a few dwarfs, but there's over seven hundred festivals in Spain where they throw goats out of church belfries.

JOSH: So, it's been a really political summer for you, what with the dwarf-tossing and goat-tossing...

CORA: Yeah.

JOSH: I think you're perfect for this party!

(He whips the invitation into her face—and we do a quick cross-fade to J.P. stopping John as he walks quickly lugging an armful of books.)

J.P.: Johnny! Hey, John! How's it going?

JOHN: What? What do you want?

J.P.: I like what you said in World History today, about Jesus and everything. You can really fill in those Dead Sea scrolls and things, all that background you've got.

JOHN: You've got to be kidding—you looked spaced out. I don't get it. One day you're Turrett's Syndrome, then you're brain dead.

J.P.: Hey, that's how I look when something fascinates me. I like it the way you always talk.

JOHN: You're putting me on. *(Starts to leave.)*

J.P.: No, I was really interested in that parable you told about Jesus and the alibaster ointment.

(John stops.)

J.P.: What kid in their right mind is going to know about alibaster ointment?

JOHN: *(comes back, looks at J.P. suspiciously)* I heard you telling Joanna Wislewski you thought I was a religious freak—and you used to throw M&M's at me. I always thought you were a big sneak.

J.P.: Hey, I'm serious. I just wanted to get it straight—what happened? Jesus accepted some of this expensive alabaster ointment from Mary Magdalene. You're great when you're frank. Jesus used some of the ointment, was that it?

JOHN: Right. He had it rubbed on his skin.

J.P.: And then Judas, the bag man for the disciples, said, "Hey, Jesus, you shouldn't have used it on yourself—we could have sold the alabaster ointment." See, I mean, I was really riveted.

JOHN: Yeah.

J.P.: But what does it mean?

JOHN: You really want to know?

J.P.: Yeah.

JOHN: It's symbolic of personal need. See, Jesus told Judas—He said, "I used it on myself because I am deserving." It was something he needed, just some little thing for himself. Do you know what it's like to give, give, give—and then need just something for yourself? You just stop and say I need. I need something!

J.P.: Oh, sure Johnny. You know a lot of kids admire how cerebral you are. *(He whips out an invitation.)* How'd you like to go to a party? *(Quick cross cutting with spots to focus on the Dracula Musical Auditions. Ann and Betsy sing alternating snippets of songs.)*

ANN: *(in her spot, singing) So you met someone who*
set you back on your heels,
goody, goody...

BETSY: *(in her spot) Bei mir bist du schon*
Please let me explain—means
that you're grand.

ANN: *(practicing dance steps) So you met someone*
and now you know
how it feels,
goody, goody.

JIMMY: *(sneaking up behind Ann)* Hey, you've really got a great voice, Ann.

ANN: Thanks. I mean, that's really nice of you to say that, it really is.

JIMMY: Great audition. I hope Mr. Shaffer gives you the part of Dracula's wife. We'd look good together. I was sorry to hear about your older brother. He was good in computer class.

ANN: Yeah, like he was the only inside trader at Merrill-Lynch, right. They gave him six months, I mean, my God, they give suspended sentences to murderers, right?

JIMMY: How's your sister doing? I liked that article she wrote in the *Sea Hawk Gazette* about how boys who wear pointed shoes make better lovers.

ANN: She dropped out—gave birth with dolphins down in the Keys.

JIMMY: Is your younger brother still a Scientologist?

ANN: No, I can't keep up with him ever since he dropped out of school. You know how kids are. One month he's searching for a Venezuelan Terror Blob—the next he'd joined a dig for Hitler's corpse.

JIMMY: He was cool—the only teenage psychic I ever knew. You still hoping to get into Cornell Veterinary School and become a pet therapist?

ANN: Oh, yeah—I figure, got to have a dream, right? Got to have a dream!

(Lighting cross cuts to Betsy.)

BETSY: *(singing) I could say Bella, Bella,*
even say vunderbar,
each language only helps me tell you
how grand you are!

STEVIE: Are you still seeing a psychiatrist, Betsy?

BETSY: Yes...

STEVIE: Was it because of your grandfather?—he was such a nice old man—it must have been a terrible shock, I mean his will—when you found out he wanted to be buried in a pink party dress.

BETSY: I don't think my father would have had a sex change operation under ordinary circumstances. I've been trying to work it out with the shrink, you know, about my parents—how sweet and simple they were running their Mom & Pop candy store, and then one day I come home and find out it's a Mom & Mom shop.

STEVIE: I guess that could freak any kid out.

BETSY: What made me really need psychiatric treatment was when my mom joined a softball team of women who used to be men—and they were playing against a team of men who used to be women. And I was sitting in the stands watching these big women playing these little ittie bittie men—and I felt like I was on Mars! I didn't know who I was anymore.

(Spots on both couples.)

ANN & BETSY: *Goody, goody for you*
goody goody for me
and I hope you're satisfied,
you rascal you!

(Jimmy and Stevie both whip out invitations for Ann and Betsy—then Blackout. Ulie's voice comes over speakers, amplified—echo chamber.)

ULIE'S VOICE: Maureen! Maureen!

(Dim light grows as Ulie runs across the limbo to Maureen. He's got the collection container—she's got the bag of taco chips.)

ULIE: I think we've got to get back to the party now. Peter and Jessica are going to call!

MAUREEN: We don't have enough money yet. Vinnie'll really get ticked off.

ULIE: Hey, just one shot and I've got enough for your movie—and to take Vinnie out for quesadillas. *(He gives Maureen the container.)*

MAUREEN: *(taking out money)* How'd you get so much? Did you hit a house where they have a priest for a son?

ULIE: No—I told them I was helping out my sister who has to raise money to take her organized crime boyfriend to the movies—so she makes believe she's collecting for Catholic Charities—but there's a monster that comes after her in her head that's trying to drive her crazy, so she has to crinkle a bag of taco chips in her ear to keep it away—and so they gave me fifty bucks!

MAUREEN: This is wonderful, Ulie.

ULIE: You've got to tell them the truth, Maureen. There're a lot of good people around, you just tell them the truth.

(Maureen looks away, distracted Ulie sits next to her.)

ULIE: What's the monster look like, Maureen—what does it look like?

MAUREEN: I don't want you to know.

ULIE: I want to know—it might be hereditary.

MAUREEN: I don't want you worrying…

ULIE: Just tell me what it's like. What do you see in your head?

MAUREEN: I see…a carnival. That's what I usually see.

ULIE: A carnival?

MAUREEN: That's how it begins.

ULIE: Carnival's are fun.

MAUREEN: It starts pretty…lights, and rides, cotton candy and a kind of tinkling music…

ULIE: Merry-go-round music?

MAUREEN: Yeah. And a midway, and a Whip and a Ferris wheel and lots of people. An arcade and barkers and waffle stands…and souvenirs…

ULIE: It sounds beautiful.

MAUREEN: It does, it looks beautiful at first…but then something happens…

ULIE: What?

MAUREEN: I notice it's different...

ULIE: Is it like a dream, Maureen?

MAUREEN: I mean, there are lights and rides...but the merry-go-round is turning backwards...it doesn't go forward. When I look close at everything, it's all spinning, turning—backwards. That's when I start to get frightened. I see trees, mangrove trees are there—and their roots are growing upwards. And there are fish. Strange glistening fish that can climb the trees. And then suddenly, I realize the carnival is in a swamp. A swamp where a tiger is loose. A tiger that's after me...it's after everyone. It's like tigers I read about in a Bengal swamp—where they have to drink salt water and it changes their brains...and when I look at the people in the swamp carnival, I see they're all frightened, too. They have babies on their shoulders, and they're holding balloons, and everyone knows the tiger is after them. It's a tiger that won't attack if you're looking at it—and so I start to run, I run spinning, trying to look everywhere so the tiger won't get me. And I see they're all wearing smiles painted on them, masks to fool the tiger—but I'm the only one who knows the tiger's on to their trick. I want to cry out, "The masks don't work anymore! They don't work!" but the sounds get caught in my throat and they sound like...

ULIE: Let me hear the sound, Maureen.

MAUREEN: They sound like... (*She lets out two soft, but high-pitched cries from her soul—and they capture the terror of the monster which stalks us all.*)

ULIE: Can't anyone stop the tiger, Maureen?

MAUREEN: I don't know. I don't know.

(*The spot on Maureen and Ulie fades to black. Suddenly, a strobe hits the stage as the party bursts into full swing. Ann, John, Betsy, and Cora look sensational in party clothes. Jimmy, Josh, Stevie, and J.P. bang bongo drums as the strobe picks up speed and driving, pulsing Instrumental Music kicks the party into its highest gear.*)

(*We glimpse all our characters front and center in different moments—Josh doing a wild dance, Jimmy and Ann flash dancing, Cora, Wendy, Gabby, Betsy—all of them, even Maureen and Ulie [returned to the party] letting it all hang out.*)

(*The strobe stops as suddenly as it started, and the characters continue the normal chaos of a party—as the music ends.*)

GABBY: Hey, where is everybody else? Where are the others? I thought you said forty or fifty were coming.

DAN: It's a start. The word gets out. Next party'll be packed. It takes time, you know.

MAUREEN: It's time for them to call. Were you getting calls, were there a lot of kids calling?

DAN: Hey, they're probably busy, between races. By the time they post the wins, you know, how much time they got to figure out what they're going to bet next—they have to look the horses over.

DAVE: They said they'd call. They had that look in their eyes like they were really going to. They were eating hot dogs...

MAUREEN: Did Vinny call while we were out? If he stops by, I don't want any cracks, okay. He takes it out on me, you know.

(Jimmy circulates, distributing cans of Coke.)

GABBY: Nobody called. Can't somebody send out for some food? Can't you send out? One lousy pizza, anything? Chinese?

WENDY: I'll go to White Castle, you want to go to White Castle? I'm not doing Burger King or Roy Rogers—no composite chicken.

DAN: Come on, get another tune on there. That English one with the guys imitating Megadeth...

MAUREEN: Can't you play something slow? *(To Jimmy)* Where's the Diet Coke? Somebody drank the cooking sherry, you know.

JIMMY: There's 7-Up, you want a 7-Up? The ice is out. Whoever's eating the ice, cut it out. No ice eating.

JOHN: *(approaching Gabby)* You want to dance? I see you rollerblading all the time. I saw you fall. Sounded like you cracked your knee. Dance, okay?

GABBY: *(frozen, not looking at John)* I'm sorry, I think I'm coming down with a blood clot. Maybe I'll dance later, I never know what I'm going to do. *(She urgently signals Wendy to join her.)*

ANN: *(to Dave)* I don't understand, Dave, your parents are on some kind of a trotting vacation? They go away, and you're going to have parties every week?

STEVIE: Hey, don't worry about it. They're off, they won something, filled out something at Tower Records—won a contest thing.

(The faxing sequence kicks into action as Dan scoots to the machine, along with Maureen, Dave, and Ulie.)

DAN: *(taking charge of the incoming message)* Everything's cool. It's not going to be a call.

BETSY: They've been gone two months? My mothers were gambling in Puerto Rico on a junket. Sent me a card of Morro Castle.

CORA: My Mom's addicted to video poker. She gets her paycheck and she's out of town. She's like Miss Lotto Fever. It used to be a lot of Keno.

DAN: *(taking first page from fax tray)* It's a cover sheet, Track Fax—yeah, Peter and Jessica. They're still in Ohio. We forgot they shut the pay phones off at the track.

ULIE: *(jumping in)* Can I read the message sheet, can I? How can you tell it's from them? Where do you look?

DAN: Nope. I got it. I told you it'd be a fax. Lookin' good, lookin' good...

MAUREEN: *(attempting to pull Ulie away)* Come on, Ulie, I'll teach you how to Merengue. Vinnie loves to Merengue.
(Ulie stays focused on fax machine.)

JIMMY: What'd they say? What's it going to be, like a whole thing?

JOSH: Yeah, what'd they say?

DAN: *(taking the second in-coming sheet from the machine)* Not too much, I mean this stuff costs—they're not going to send a book...*(reading)* Dear kids, we're sorry to have to write this...*(he laughs)* It's not going to be bad...

ULIE: Did Mommy write it? Who wrote it?

DAVE: Why couldn't they have called? They could've called before.

ANN: *(to Jimmy)* What's going on? Why would they go to Ohio, why aren't they at the Meadowlands?

DAN: Hey, they're having a good time. It's cool. *(Continuing reading) We're not coming home. We're sorry Dave came after us. Please don't look for us anymore. (Dan puts the message down and starts laughing)* We can read it later. They're just doing their thing. Get some music in, let's keep the party going...it's the usual...

GABBY: *(takes up the message sheet—continues reading from it) We're sorry we ever had children.*

WENDY: Don't read it in front of everyone. I mean, you don't have to wave our laundry, you know...

GABBY: Who cares? Half their parents are psychos, too. This is not a very nice message, you know. I mean, it sucks...

DAN: *(moving about the room)* Everybody does it, save up, get a wad—go to a casino and blow it—everybody does that once in a while.

GABBY: *(continuing reading) It was a mistake. We thought there was some meaning. We thought we'd all like each other and need each other. That there was some point to it all.*

DAN: Who wants a drink? Jimmy, go out and get some chips and dip. They're like putting us on…it's a joke…

GABBY: *(continuing reading) Your mother and I don't like each other anymore, either. It's all fake. Everything's fake. At least here we forget…the horses go into the homestretch and we get excited…*

DAN: Dad probably just had a couple of beers too many. Remember how he used to say God was on vacation? Remember that? God's in Martinique, remember his little joke?

GABBY: *Ulie was okay, but we know he'll soon turn into what the rest of you are. You're users. You're losers. Gimme. Gimme. Please don't even look for us. We're changing our names. Like we said, don't look for us. Sorry. (Gabby puts down the message. For a moment we see how devastated everyone is—except Dan who laughs.)*

DAN: *(putting on the music)* So, they had problems. The only problem we've got is to get this party going again. Come on, let's dance. *(He starts dancing.)* Come on, Ann. Maybe you want to sing. What's that dance you always do, that thing to Gershwin?

ANN: I've got to be going.

CORA: Me, too.

DAN: It's early. Betsy, let's dance.

BETSY: I've got some homework I've got to do.

DAN: Hey, it's great music. Somebody dance. They're coming back, Peter and Jessica—it's just a thing, it's all going to change—they're good guys…*(Dan jokingly takes the Mom mannequin out of the wheelchair, starts dancing around the room with it.)* Look, Mom, I'm dancing! Get this party going! Let's get it cookin'! Come on everybody! They were just fooling around. Dance. Hey, Gabby, grab a dummy and dance…yeah, come on…

(He grabs Dad Mannequin and throws it toward Gabby. Everyone sees Dan's starting to lose it. Maureen reaches out to him—when Dan explodes, releases his rage against the dummy. He starts to punch it, rough it up, throws it onto the floor. He starts kicking it. Dave and Maureen rush to pull him off, and he crumbles weeping. No one moves for a moment.)

ULIE: *(angrily, crossing to Dan, Dave, and Maureen, crying out, breaking our hearts)* I want our family! I want it! I want it!

(The stunned party guests back away. The rest of the family doesn't know

what to do. Wendy goes to Ulie, trying to comfort him but Ulie pulls away from her—as the lighting dims a couple of notches on Dan and the center action. As the actors freeze, we hear the sound of a bell from a starting gate at the race track, followed by a large crowd cheering. The cheering fades into an echo. Music: Mama Cass singing first few bars of "Dream a Little Dream" as Betsy comes down center. The others follow into the Chorus mode.)

BETSY: *And so the tale is ending.*

CORA: *This sighting in the family Archipelago,*

ANN: *Imps of Darkness,*

JOHN: *Night herons and cranes...*

JIMMY: *Flying above the quakes and madness.*

BETSY: *Wondering where will be our next resting place.*

J.P.: *Are we babies set adrift among the reeds and marshes and streams?*

STEVIE: *Like some countries still do with female babies...*

MAUREEN: *Children who were burdens or were prophesied to return one day and kill their fathers and inherit their thrones.*

ANN: *Children of destiny.*

GABBY: *Children sent forth to seek fleeces that didn't exist.*

ULIE: *Children left behind.*

WENDY: *Children sent under the waters.*

(Dan, Maureen, Dave, and Gabby lift the two mannequins high like bodies at a funeral. Ulie, Wendy, Stevie, and J.P. join the family, a procession. The others gather around.)

DAVE: *Will we rock the infants born in petrie dishes?*

MAUREEN: *How can they patent our very genes?*

DAN: *GM babies with bar codes on their heads.*

JOSH: *Owning our guts, our greatest dreams...*

GABBY: *We've left behind our fragile Eden, and wait to see:*

WENDY: *Are we ocean travelers?*

ULIE: *Shape-changers?*

ALL: *Or merely human on our journey to the stars?*
Were the parents naughty in the time of Oprah-speak,
Or was it the children who were naughty as can be?
Who was it that caused this great transfiguring?
Or was it all a virtual reality?
(A sharp golden light, etches, freezes our characters onto our retinas as Mama Cass' "Dream a Little Dream" grows louder. Go to darkness, ending the play.)

END OF PLAY

VOICES
FROM YOUNG ACTORS

What follows are excerpts from the writing of some of the young people who were involved with the first productions of these plays. In one case we've included selections from the journal of one of the actors who had been asked to keep a record of her reactions to the process during the actual rehearsal period. The others were asked to reflect on the experience after their particular project concluded. Since this book covers a three-year period, some of the young people have moved on to college and advanced professional training programs. In keeping with our mission, we feel that the reactions of the young people involved are essential to our creation and to our understanding of what value remains. After all, it was the need for a young point of view that provided our first impulse to begin the commission of new plays at the Young Conservatory.

DANTON CHAR
Age 20

Played multiple roles in *Class Action*

Everything I have ever heard said about originating a new character, that it is frustrating, heartrending; that you weep and howl, tearing out wads of your own hair, kicking like in a temper tantrum, proved to be absolutely true the first time I did it. This was not because it was a particularly painful process. In fact, in retrospect, it was a lot of fun. No, creating a new character was exasperating because I could not cheat.

I do not mean to say that before this experience I was corrupt, or perverse in my methods of scene work. I had, however, gotten used to playing the texts that are normally given to young actors. Mortimer, in *Arsenic and Old Lace,* is a wonderful part, but ask any kid who ever played it and we will all tell you that the whole extent of our research and character work for the role involved renting the Cary Grant movie. This works; people would tell me how good the scene was because I had gotten the character right. But at 15 and 16 this started to become annoying. My primary responsibility as a young actor seemed to be to look cute on stage, not to tell the truth.

Having new plays to act in, ones especially written for actors my age, broke all my falsehood down. The fact that they were new plays forced me to be original in the creation of my individual characters. Too, the characters in these plays were like me, people whose eyes I could see through or at least look into. In both *Ascension Day* and *Class Action,* I became an actor rather than just a performer. Through the words of Timothy Mason and Brad Slaight, I reached to touch a new platform of acting, a real one. Throughout this stretch, Craig Slaight's guidance supported me, coached me, and kept me from falling. I owe him, and these playwrights, such gratitude for helping me to first see, and encouraging me to first try, the craft of creating truth on stage.

ANDREW COHEN
Age 16

Played Josh in *Every Seventeen Minutes the Crowd Goes Crazy!*

Go into any arena, stadium, auditorium, theatre, etc. Stop, take a look around, notice your surroundings, there are seats scrunched together like young grass paying full attention to the sun. Each and every seat faces a lifeline where jobs and lives are performed nonstop. They cry for your patience and imagery, "Look at me and feel what I must feel, give me what you must offer and more, for I will give you as much, ten fold." Never will those cries vary, never will they cease. As an actor, un or experienced, there will always be that memory. Be it your first line, that look on another face, the reaction from a patron. Today, and for my life, I won't forget the chance I had, and the chance others had with me.

Where else can you be yourself and still be another person? Athletics, professional or not revolve around costumes that make that a team one. Their helmets lining each sideline like a wave to their height. If one player misses a play, another enters and makes the play. Just like that. In theatre, there will never be a playbook and a missed play. Sure mistakes will occur, theatre isn't above reality you know! It is reality, well done or not. Supported or not.

As in all life actions, motion and response are parlayed in different ways. Between two people you can find that difference in reaction. Over one and a half billion, or so, reactions live on this planet, and that's just a reaction to a single action. So put everyone on stage and pay attention to their part, it's weaved throughout each of your fellow actors, it's giving that puzzle piece and makes it whole, and able to pump. Some just get the chance to literally go onto a stage and be that character, the one living in your playwright's mind. A mind, if I might say that has enriched and solidified many, many patrons, putting pen to paper and shipping happiness and respect, importance and sympathy, and the always challenging, love and its cold war opponent hate.

The brilliant telling of a story has got to be one of life's most difficult projects. And in life you can be sure of at least one story, one attention getter, one published work...your story, for it's plot, characters, setting, situations and conclusion are real, just as real as a play, a well done, well written, well directed one, with an odd title like *Every Seventeen Minutes the Crowd Goes Crazy!* And maybe it will be written by Paul Zindel, or a writer who tells wonderful stories of those experiences in life that baffle the best of clinical psychologists...yeah, or maybe only Paul Zindel. In any case the clock's bell could just not ring for me. I'll stay and not break that wonderful time. I don't know who would. Thank you.

ADAM COSTELLO
Age 18

Played Klute in *Reindeer Soup* and Dave in *Every Seventeen Minutes the Crowd Goes Crazy!*

Only moments after I returned from a weeklong sojourn in the Sierra's the summer after my ninth grade year, my mother told me that Craig Slaight had called and asked if I wished to be a part of the Performance Workshop New Play that summer. Not truly knowing what was in store for me, I said "Sure Mom. Sounds cool. What's for dinner?"

What was for dinner was a magical experience that I was fortunate enough to be involved not only that summer, but also the summer after my senior year. It was the experience of performing a work for the first time ever, anywhere. The experience is one that every student of theater, and indeed every theater professional, should be given the chance to take part in. Unfortunately this is not the case, but the Young Conservatory at ACT does give some lucky students the chance to witness, and even take part in the birth of a play.

The first step in the birthing process was meeting the fathers. These were two wonderful men, Joe Pintauro and Paul Zindel. I have no doubt that they could have written their plays without the Director Craig Slaight, the actors, or the technicians who all helped them. But, by letting all of us into their minds, they achieved something that few plays reach. That is, a play with two parents. The father was the writer, the mother was everyone else involved, and the child was a wonder.

I shall speak of my more recent experience because of its freshness in my mind, but my first New Play was amazing as well. The child that was born last summer, the only child with two parents who loved it, was as much an ensemble experience as I have ever taken part in. Ensemble may be a vague concept for some, for it is not something that can be described. Rather, it is an experience, and emotion, a power which is felt when a group of people become one entity, striving toward one common goal. During *Every Seventeen Minutes the Crowd Goes Crazy!* the ensemble was so strong that it was almost overwhelming. The day after the final performance I was to leave for college, and instead of becoming excited at the thought, I began to dread it, for it would mean the loss of the many friends which I had made and had been brought close to by the play.

I miss you Joe Pintauro. I miss you Craig Slaight. I miss you Paul Zindel. I miss you *Reindeer Soup* and *Every Seventeen Minutes the Crowd Goes Crazy!* I miss you, all of my fellow actors. And yet I am happy, for my memories of the New Play Experience, the Birth, and the Ensemble will remain with me forever. I rejoice that there are more New Plays to come, so that the students of the future may also give life to a play which has never before been seen.

KEVIN CROOK
Age 17

Played Davis in *The Less Than Human Club* and Dan in *Every Seventeen Minutes the Crowd Goes Crazy!*

I was sitting in front of my computer trying to think of some epic start to this like "The Glory of the theater came alive in mine eyes as I stepped into my new born role." But I came to realize that whatever opening sentence I could construct, no matter how beautiful sounding, there is no way I could fully sum up my feelings about being in a commissioned play. I can say this: *It was really really fun!!!!* It's not only doing a play for the first time, it's having the playwright there and having people around you, all the same age and joining in the same amazing experience with you. I'll try to explain it though: Take the feeling that you get when you're backstage and about to go on, and you have to go to the bathroom really bad, and your heart has changed it's location from your chest to your throat and adrenaline has wired your entire system, then stretch that feeling over a five-week time span. That's what being in a commissioned play is like.

I was lucky enough to experience two commissioned plays and go through different experiences with two *amazing* playwrights: Tim Mason and Paul Zindel. It was great to experience two sides to the process of writing the play. Tim had finished the first draft of *The Less Than Human Club* in three weeks (which will never cease to amaze me) and so the basic arch of the play had been pretty much determined by the time of the first rehearsal. Paul had twenty pages of *Every Seventeen Minutes the Crowd Goes Crazy!* done by our first meeting and none of us really knew where it was going. The journey with Tim Mason was unique because we would receive new twists on scenes and additions which would change the overall feeling of the play. Some changes would work and some he would not like and it was great to watch the evolution of the play from his rough draft to final masterpiece. The Paul Zindel experience was a trip because he would show up with brand new additions to an unfinished piece and so we were always dying to know what scene would be next. It was so much fun to go through a cold read with hours-old lines and see what new things Paul had pulled out of his head.

With both playwrights, the greatest thing was to show up to rehearsal and find new pages lying in front of you. I swear it was like Christmas three times a week: To be able to just dive into those new lines and to experiment with different ways to approach your character until it all (as Paul would say) started to gel. And the biggest trip was when Paul or Tim would start taking things from our own personalities and interpretations and writing them into our character.

The awesome thing about the commissioned plays is that the teenager finally gets to play the teenager. In my high school drama class, we have books like *Great Monologues for Men* where you find some guy talking about this cocaine addiction or two men talking about the problem with being a stripper; nothing which seventeen-year-olds have really experienced. And while these are fun roles to play with (it's always fun to try to be a 85-year-old steamboat operator), there is a certain kind of truthfulness to playing a seventeen-year-old when you are that age; you really can own that character. That realism is reflected in the audience's reaction to seeing these plays. The writing is powerful, the message is powerful and the roles are powerful. The greatest feeling from doing these two plays was to look up at the end and see that you've made a connection, not just with your peers and not just the adults but everyone in the theater. Everyone is hit by the message that we've carried.

I can't even talk about what it's like at the end of it all. I'm still wearing an ACT withdrawal patch on my arm that says, *Every Seventeen Minutes the Crowd Goes Crazy!* You become so close with your cast so quickly it's like you're all family by the end. You eat together, party together, chill together and then it just stops. That's hard. But the experience (I hate to get cheesy...sorry) from doing this, both years, are beyond any other thing I've done in my life.

CARMEN MOLINARI
Age 17

Played Chelo in *Eddie Mundo Edmundo* and Cora in *Every Seventeen Minutes the Crowd Goes Crazy!*

"Two minutes," whispered Craig to the actors in the wings. It was pitch dark backstage and I, along with my fellow cast members, could not see a thing. We could only hear the distant chatting, hushing, and laughing from our awaiting, anxious audience. The butterflies in our stomachs were growing painful but we were too overjoyed and emotional to let that stop us from tripping over each other as we struggled to meet hands. We needed to kiss and embrace each other before our cue came that would take us through that imaginary door in the wings and lead us to the brand new world of our play, a play we created through weeks of rigorous rehearsal. We were not scared, but ready because we knew we had the guide of a never-before-performed script and the genius of an incredible director.

I tried to hold back tears as I held one of my cast mates, Nick Hongola, in my arms. Nick, like the rest of my cast, became more than just a fellow cast member during the process of this play, but a part of me, like family. Then, as I let him go, I was flooded with memories of this whole unique experience.

I remembered how my heart skipped a beat after receiving a phone call from the director telling me that I was chosen to perform in Paul Zindel's *Every Seventeen Minutes the Crowd Goes Crazy!*, the Young Conservatory's newly commissioned play. Two years earlier, I had played Chelo in the New Plays Program commission *Eddie Mundo Edmundo* by Lynne Alvarez. How nervous and intimidated I felt as I looked around the reading table the first day of rehearsal, at all the talented faces, including Pulitzer Prize–winning playwright, Paul Zindel, and one of my mentors and our director, Craig Slaight.

I'll never forget the excitement, that first day, of holding in my hands the unfinished newborn piece, that had been specifically written for us, and knowing that the ending to the play would be inspired by us during the course of our rehearsal process. The frustration, dedication and glory in developing my role into more than just lines in a script, but a living, breathing, individual was overwhelming and exciting. I knew that when it was over I would miss the cast bonding over french fries at

Wendy's and shopping at the new Virgin Mega-store after intense rehearsals.

Finally it came time for me and the rest of the cast and crew to put all this hard work, love, and passion on stage. What a victory it was to have performed that night in the world premiere of our play with such true conviction and reality. And, oh how I dreaded taking my last bow and saying good-bye to my cast family! How could I say good-bye to those two beautiful plays, and the people that made me grow so much as an actress and as a person? But I will always feel honored and very thankful that I was able to be a part of something so powerful and amazing as the Young Conservatory's New Plays Program.

CHELSEA PERETTI
Age 17

Played Gabby in *Every Seventeen Minutes the Crowd Goes Crazy!*

Whenever I open to the first page of a play and see the original cast list, a nervous, excited energy runs through me. I know that the names I am staring at are those of the first actors to speak the written words of the playwright. I know that they have already completed the process that I am about to begin. This opportunity to create the physical manifestation of a new character has always seemed both a grave responsibility and a marvelous honor. I was eternally grateful then when I was chosen, along with fourteen other teens, to participate in the original production of *Every Seventeen Minutes the Crowd Goes Crazy!* by the Pulitzer Prize–winner, Paul Zindel.

It was a unique and intense experience for a plethora of reasons, one being my immediate fondness for Paul Zindel. Mr. Zindel was down-to-earth, supportive, and consistently mirthful during the two weeks of rehearsals he attended, and later, at our performances. He listened with an open mind to all the actors' ideas concerning his script. Each day, with the often surprising and consistently moving and hilarious new pages he brought in, we were reminded of his creative expertise as a writer. Often, an actor could not successfully complete the reading of a line because he was giggling hysterically along with the cast. In this process, the material never ceased to be new to all of us which added a refreshing, and a nerve-wracking element. In addition, the cast was very close. Our director, Craig Slaight, encouraged this closeness, as well as a friendly relationship with him. Despite the affectionate relationships we all formed, Craig insisted that we maintain a professional atmosphere during rehearsal time, a decision that I appreciated.

I became so accustomed to the routine of migration from my home in Oakland to the studio in San Francisco, interaction with friends and colleagues, warm-ups, intense rehearsals, and finally performances, that I went through withdrawal after the termination of the project. I kept awakening with the urge to run onto the next arriving BART train and to dash back into the Hastings Studio to learn more about myself as an actor. I yearned to slip back into the lace skirt and short black pleated skirt of Gabby, my character, and speak her words again. My participation in the play had become like breathing to me, like eating. Each day

I would consider a new aspect of Gabby or her speech. Conversations and situations in my post-show life inevitably reminded me of a line from the play, one which I would restrain myself from reciting. I knew that only someone who had been involved in the production would be able to understand.

The most important aspect of participating in the Performance Workshop was the sense that the cast was a unit. We shared our characters' family histories and analyses, our food, our stories, our anxieties and our victories. At all times we felt we had the support of every other cast member. We were a friendly and focused team with a common goal. I realized what a powerful ensemble we had become after our first performance, when we all went to a lounge on the uppermost floor of a popular nearby hotel. Joining us were mutual friends from other acting classes at ACT who had enjoyed watching the show as much as we had enjoyed performing it. We ordered various exotic virgin drinks and began chattering away as we had chattered continually over the past several weeks.

Eventually a soulful oldies group began to sing. We all got out of our chairs and began to dance and clap and sing along with them. There was no embarrassment or fear; we had seen each other in awkward or vulnerable positions already during rehearsals. Two people had pulled the youngest member of the cast, Ulie, onto their shoulders and were dancing around frantically. Excitement and positive energy exuded from our very pores. Our dancing souls had found in the lounge rather easily what we had worked to find with each other onstage: trust, rhythm, timing, and natural flow.

PAUL SHIKANY
Age 20

Played Eddie in *Eddie Mundo Edmundo* and was Assistant Director
for *The Less Than Human Club*

As theater artists we are compelled to search for truth and clarity in
the life that is constantly occurring around us. We consider the theater
to be one place where all aspects of life may be freely explored. This freedom extends itself to the exploration of life from the perspective of
young people, and with the New Plays program, those of us fortunate
enough to participate are given that opportunity firsthand. In a creative,
sharing, and exciting atmosphere, seasoned theater artists collaborate
with students to create plays that are rich and honest.

The role of Eddie in 1993's *Eddie Mundo Edmundo* was my third
with the program, and as always a challenge in creation and performance. The presence of playwright Lynne Alvarez early in the process
was a tremendous help in character development. An understanding of
the creator's thoughts about the play is an asset to a performer's interpretation. Lynne's support greatly aided us in making honest and valuable discoveries throughout the process. I look back on the creation of
"Eddie" now as an inspiring experience with many lessons learned;
lessons about the process of play development and the sense of ensemble so vital to the success of the production. Perhaps most of all, I see
this production as a milestone in learning to value the entire process of
play creation, to see the joy and importance of the messages we strive so
diligently to tell.

In the summer of 1994, with a year of college under my belt and
the knowledge accumulated through multiple roles in new plays, I returned to the program as an assistant director for Tim Mason's *The Less
Than Human Club*. My work in this production included "traditional"
assistant's work, such as sharing my own perceptions with the director.
In addition, the added experience of being a veteran to the program enabled me to better understand the perspective of the actors. This helped
me to develop close friendships with the members of the ensemble, and
at the same time aid in direction of the play. This combination—working closely in rehearsal with the actors and getting to know and understand them as people became an important aid in helping to move the
play forward in development. I consider this production to be one of the

most educational I have been a part of. *The Less Than Human Club* helped me to understand the process in its entire scope, from the perspective of a director as well as an actor. In addition, working with actors in a situation I had recently been in myself was enlightening and exciting. It was an honor to help "pass on" the joy of the program to other actors.

The New Plays program has become a powerful institution, powerful in the sense that it is a unique and truly joyous environment where the voices of young people are allowed and encouraged to be heard. My participation in the program is no longer an active part of my life, and in a removed, more objective mode of thought I have often wondered what the "secret" is; what makes this program so special. From my own thoughts as well as discussion with fellow participants, I feel that the "secret," if such a thing exists, is this value that is placed on the youthful voice. We are living in a world where the emotions and fears of the young are too often ignored and undervalued. There are still, as always, the dreams of youth, the joys, hopes, and discoveries. These feelings are an integral part of the experience of being young. Yet more and more in our own time, humanity finds itself grappling with increasingly more difficult and complicated problems, problems entirely beyond the understanding of adults, to say nothing of children. In this era of ever-increasing isolation we are lucky to have a place where the feelings that resonate so strongly in the world of the young are shared and celebrated. In the body of plays the program has helped on its way, we have explored such diverse topics as loss, racial relations, suicide, human sexuality, and parental abandonment, as well as love, hope, magic reindeer and aliens, to name only a few. We have had the opportunity to laugh, as well as confront the very real issues that young people must face. The plays are resonant with poignancy and laughter, love and hope. I am truly fortunate to have been a part of this program. These experiences are among the most valuable and monumental of my life, and the memories and lessons learned will be a part of me always.

REBECCA WHITE
Age 17

Played Maureen in *Every Seventeen Minutes the Crowd Goes Crazy!*

Twenty-two pages lay before us, bound neatly in little notebooks. "Only twenty-two pages?" I thought. We gathered in our first of what would be many circles to read...a new play. We would be the first. The excitement was keenly tangible. We sat haphazardly around the folding tables those first few days—a tentative circle of new faces. As we listened together to a track of Craig's Mama Cass CD, I tried to imagine this play we were going to perform that as yet didn't have an ending.

Those twenty-two pages were daunting. They also were delightful frustration. Every day on BART, as we rode home, it went roughly the same way during those first weeks:

"Hey Kev, when will we get the next new pages?"

"I don't know. I keep waiting for Dan and Dave to have it out!"

"Tomorrow, you think?"

"Maybe..."

As the days passed, we got to know one another's habits and personalities through tongue twisters in warm-up circles, and through sheer hours of togetherness. We did endless improvs, learned each other's styles, and everyone got used to loaning Eli (the youngest in the group, nine-years-old) money for the vending machine.

"You don't understand, all I have is a Snickers and M&M's. All I need is 35¢ and I can get some Red Vines."

"I see..."

I came to see that they were twenty-two pages of promise. Of possibility. Those twenty-two pages were an invitation to get our hands muddy right along with Paul, and help in the creation. For the clay was wet, and still malleable. Often, I caught myself thinking, "Did I sneak in some back door? How'd I get lucky enough to be a part of this? I'm in the same room as Paul Zindel, and I don't have to call him Mr. Zindel!" I was in awe of everyone I worked with, and the ring of empty chairs—waiting to be filled—reminded me of my special privilege.

I watched each of our selves add to the creation, as Paul invited us in. Our lingo, our jives, our ideas, our personalities unmistakably found their way into the indelible final form.

"No, I think 'dork' gets used a lot more than 'dweeb'."

We all were shaping it every day, often unknowingly, sometimes in big ways, often in little:

"Paul?"

"Hmm?"

"Phil Rizutto doesn't do the Money Store commercials anymore."

"He doesn't?"

"No, they've got a new guy. It's Jim Palmer."

"Well, we'll have to get that changed…Jim Palmer you said?"

I watched an improv I did with Maureen's shrink turned into some script beyond those first twenty-two pages. And I saw a conversation about Adam's family smelted into a monologue about Dave's hippie family with the VW that vrooms.

"Our play has an ending!" I exulted as we staged the final scene, listening to the Mama Cass that was playing in the background…

"Sweet dreams till sunbeams find you, sweet dreams, and leave all worries behind you." We had done that, and I never could have foreseen the results. And when we were faxed new pages only a day before we opened, even then the creation was being hammered into perfect dimension. Through all these circles, and pages, we'd created a play, and the act of creating was equally as beautiful as the creation.

By the end, we all had played a part in Paul's process. We'd all been willing to play, and so it became our process. We'd been there and lived each step of the creation, which gave us a shared ownership in that journey. For me, it made Maureen more urgent. She was more precious to me, and I worked to bring life to every one of her words. I couldn't do any less, after watching Paul work on each one.

The rehearsals flew by. Ours was a pregnancy of only five weeks, but the work that emerged was by no means premature—after five weeks of rapid-fire changes and tumultuous thoughts in a sort of creative overdrive, it was an eloquent, charged piece, waiting to be heard.

At the end of the play, as we stood hand in hand, there was one of our circles again. But this time unfurled at each end, open, to give our work to the faces sitting captive in the dark…watching our world premiere.

KRISTIN SCHWARTZ

Kristin Schwartz, a 1994 graduate of Aragon High School in San Mateo, California, created the role of Amanda in *The Less Than Human Club* and kept a journal throughout the rehearsal process. She is now a sophomore at Oberlin College in Ohio. Here are some excerpts from her journal. (These excerpts appeared in the March, 1995 issue of *Dramatics* magazine.)

JULY 25

We read, today, through the play once…The voices work well together—bodies don't matter, the voices are right. Personalities should mingle well.

I feel more and more as if I am in deeper and deeper over my head.

JULY 27

Day two of rehearsal is over. I finished reading *Siddhartha* this morning as a prep for Amanda, and I can say that reading it was one of the most worthwhile experiences I've had. Reading *Siddhartha* was an extremely almost religious experience. Not only did it relate to me personally because Sidd's observations about time matched mine or because it matched my poem about searching for my Self, but because Tim Mason is a genius playwright.

Just the idea that *Siddhartha* is alluded to in his play adds immense universality and depth to it. Each character is a part of Siddhartha in their own way, each searching with goals in mind. Amanda is close to being Siddhartha himself as she rejects to an extent and finds childish the concerns of those she sees around her. And though their goals are not as lofty as Amanda's, they too are searching for how they fit in this world. Davis is sort of a successful Siddhartha; he knows who he is, he loves "all humanity." Mason is a genius.

I now sit across the table from him in awe, dying to tell him what I think I understand about his play.

AUGUST 2

We all danced at the start of class to cool sixties music as a warm-up. That was embarrassing. Eight actors dancing and Craig, Mr. Mason, Paul (Shikany, assistant director), and Danton (Char, playwright's assistant) watching us—NOT COOL.

Then we started our reading and went all the way through. After my three scenes with Davis, when I'm calling him on dating Kirsten, at the baboons, and after one other (scene), I think Craig just said "Nice." No direction, no "Try it again." Only, "Nice." That was exciting.

I feel a lot better about the stoned scene with Dan. I'm taking it slower, and with Craig's direction I've now got a much better grip on the scene.

I also noticed in today's reading, more of the intricacies of the play crafted by Mr. Mason. A lot of what Davis says at the start of the play is stuff he picks up from the other characters throughout the play. I thought that was cool.

AUGUST 3

Well, today was a somewhat more difficult rehearsal. We had to talk the autobiographies of our characters that we wrote for Monday's rehearsal—not read them. I could see my heartbeats through my shirt because of the way my heart was pounding with nervousness. I had a lot to say about (Amanda)—when Craig and Tim weren't putting me on the spot. When my turn came—whoosh—there went all my relatively brilliant ideas.

Re: the stage kisses—Craig announced today that we will, starting today, embrace when the script says kiss and work our way up from there. Sounds okay to me. I'm sure that by the time we get there I'll be fine with the kissing stuff.

I was politely informed by my classmates today that I smoke pot wrong, real wrong. Now I think I do it better, after watching their eager demos. What can I say? I'm an innocent...

AUGUST 6

Mr. Mason's last day at rehearsal and our first day of actual staging.

All in all a relatively good rehearsal. It's weird, but I feel like the minute I started moving I lost touch with Amanda. I also decided I have no talent whatsoever. I wish we could go back to reading around the table. I liked that part—it was safe, it was okay to royally screw up, and now it's more pressured. I don't know.

AUGUST 9

Rarely does a cast bond as successfully as *The Less Than Human*

Club. We all get along very well. We went to Oh La La! (a local coffee-house) after rehearsal and goofed around.

Day one without Tim. It was different but it was okay. Sometimes the cast gets along too well for Craig's taste. We all joke around a lot. It's hard sometimes because yeah, I want to be mature and all, but I also like goofing with everyone…This is a really great experience, I'm sorry I'll have to leave it so quickly and go off to college.

Rehearsal now is just blocking each scene. We're supposed to have everything memorized by Friday or so, lines and blocking. Ugh! Suddenly I feel like there's no time to block it all, rehearse it all, learn it all, but I guess we'll pull it off pretty well.

AUGUST 10

I think all is going well—the cast is bonding, the show is coming along.

Paul told me he's done over thirty shows in his life, including three commissions and three new plays (six new plays altogether). This is my fifth show in life. Maria (Sideris, who played Kirsten) and Lauren (Hodges, who played Julie) have agents. The thought didn't occur to me. Every now and again I feel extremely out of place, out of touch, and I feel lost, without even a goal to aim for, let alone a path to reach it. I guess that's life.

AUGUST 16

We're moving into serious rehearsal time—no breaks, we run lines when we aren't on stage. My costume fitting is scheduled for tomorrow at ACT's costume shop. That should be exciting.

Everything is going along smoothly. I feel sometimes as though we need an extra week or two of rehearsal.

AUGUST 19

Well, the second act is coming along well enough. The kisses were lame. It was pretty much like kissing my brothers or something—I really needn't have worried. The last scene is still stronger than the rest of the act. We seem to have so little energy compared with that last scene.

AUGUST 22

Day one with lights and the real set and all the sound and everything. It was really exciting. We also managed to focus as a cast, which was exciting and impressive. The show seems okay except it is still lacking what Craig calls "urgency."

I had to explain to my father tonight that rehearsals do not involve time to socialize. I had to explain to him that I was so very exhausted because a five-plus-hour rehearsal is an immense mental strain. Now my father has more respect for me and actors in general.

Well, the costumes have been chosen, the set finalized, the lighting designed…The rest is just energy and focus and luck.

AUGUST 23

Today it actually felt like a show that could potentially be good. I actually felt confident, and I found a routine for during the show that seems like it will keep me focused and enhance my performance. I have discovered that reading a book when I am not on stage helps me to focus on my character somehow—not paying attention to what I'm doing helps me do it better. Well, it worked today anyway. I was never more together as Amanda. I also learned that I don't like it when other people aren't as focused as I am, I nearly hit Mike (Smith, who played Dan) when he was being slightly goofy before our dancing scene. I wanted him to be serious and he really didn't want to.

Tonight Craig told us we're pretty darn good, and if we keep working we'll be great. Kind of neat, ain't it?

AUGUST 24

The show is a show now. Tomorrow, Tim comes back and he'll see our dress rehearsal. That's pretty cool, I guess. Having him there will be kind of nerve-wracking, but I guess he's supportive so it's okay. I'm really looking forward to actually having an audience out there. Half of theatre is the audience and the rapport between the characters and the audience. It's not quite right without it.

AUGUST 25

Well, Tim came back and he loved it. Craig claims to have shed a tear during our dress rehearsal today. I guess we're pretty good.

We all welcomed Tim back with open arms (lots of hugs). We joked with him as if he'd never been gone. It was neat to have him back. It gives you a sense of completeness and sharing. We met on July 25 with the man and his ideas. We worked together for two weeks, and then he gave us his baby to take care of. Now we've given to him the reality that was in his mind, the child grown up. It's a pretty amazing process if you think about it.

AUGUST 27

We rocked today. Our afternoon show was called by Tim and Craig "our best yet." Our evening show was better. Tonight, as Domenic (Manchester, who played Clinton) said, even the blood worked! Tonight five weeks of work burst forth in the glory that is theatre. We were right on all night. It was great.

I plan to keep in touch with Paul, Domenic, Mike, and Lauren, along with Craig and Tim. I guess my hand will hurt all year from all the letters I have to write. But that's okay with me. This has been a great experience. I couldn't have dreamed up a better one.

*The plays in this volume were originally produced with the
generous support from the LEF Foundation and The Fred Gellert
Foundation, at the American Conservatory Theater.*